THE SIRIUS PUPPY TRAINING MANUAL

# How To Teach
# A New Dog Old Tricks

Ian Dunbar PhD, MRCVS

James & Kenneth
PUBLISHERS

How To Teach A New Dog Old Tricks
by Ian Dunbar

First published in 1981 by Sirius Puppy Training
Second Edition: James & Kenneth Publishers, 1991
Third Edition published in the USA by:

> James & Kenneth Publishers
> 2140 Shattuck Avenue #2406
> Berkeley, California 94704
> (800) 784-5531

> James & Kenneth - Canada
> 2353 Belyea Street
> Oakville, Ontario L6L 1N8
> (905) 469-1555 ext 3

> James & Kenneth - UK
> P O Box 111, Harpenden
> Hertfordshire, AL5 2GD
> 01582 715765

IBSN 1-888047-06-2

*For my old English teacher Mr. Johns, who encouragingly said, "Dunbar you can't write, you never could write and you never will be able to write!"*

*And for Mother and Dad, who thought there was still hope and so gave me a Thesaurus and dictionary. Thank you!*

**Photo Credits**
Diana Robinson: pages 37, 75, 120, 123, 127, 131 and 146
Linda Carlson: pages 16 and 101
Neal Morrison: pages 93
Jennifer Bassing: page 8
Jamie Dunbar CEDHOP K9-Games: page 159
Thank you all!
All other photographs were taken by the author.

Front Cover Dog Oso trained and handled by Dr.Linda Carlson

Front Cover Design by Quark & Bark Late Night Graphics Co. Inc.
Back Cover Design by Montessaurus Media
Back Cover Photographs by Neal Morrison and Veronica Charlwood

Printed in the USA

# TABLE OF CONTENTS

*The Dog and The Doctor*

# Dialogue between the Doctor and the Dog

Between veterinarian Dr. Ian Dunbar
and his Alaskan Malamute, Omaha Beagle

Dr.: "Why do dogs misbehave?"

Dog: "Who's to say we misbehave. We dogs hold that our behavior is quite exemplary."

Dr.: "Okay. We, the people, think dogs misbehave. Let's be a little more precise then and ask; why do dogs chase, chew, dig, snarl, snap, bark and bite?"

Dog: "Largely because we're dogs, I suppose. Surely you'd be a mite surprised if we flew, did crosswords, kept bones in the fridge, mooed and miaowed, and urged lawyers to sue our adversaries?"

Dr.: "Okay, okay! Granted, all dogs' activities are quite normal and necessary ingredients of the natural canine behavior repertoire. So, it's not so much that the behaviors are abnormal in themselves but rather the behaviors are simply inappropriate in the domestic setting."

Dog: "Well, yes and no - I guess it depends on your perspective. We dogs do not necessarily consider our behavior inappropriate even. On the contrary, a Yorkie friend of mine considers deep-pile carpet the cutting edge in domestic toilets - quite the most perfect place to pee in the entire household. And old Jack Russell willingly admits that a freshly tilled annual border offers ideal terra softa for excavations (considering the delicate nature of his paws, softened from years of domestic living)."

Dr.: "So, correct me if I'm wrong. What you're saying is that dog behaviors are perfectly normal and natural..."

Dog: "And necessary!"

Dr.: "...and necessary in the wild..."

Dog: "And in the domestic setting!"

Dr.: "...and in the domestic setting."

Dog: "And so the onus lies with the owner to provide and indicate mutually acceptable and appropriate outlets for our necessary doggy activities, otherwise..."

9

Dr.:    "Otherwise?"

Dog:    "...otherwise we are forced to improvise in our quest for occupational therapy to pass the time of day."

Dr.:    "And no doubt you'll get it wrong. Right?"

Dog:    "Right! And then we get punished for breaking rules that we didn't even know existed."

Dr.:    "That's not fair."

Dog:    "Well, it hardly makes us happy."*

(*As a breed, malamutes are renowned for their biting, litotic sarcasm.)

Dr.:    "Hmmmm! Have you ever tried explaining to your owners that you are unaware of any wrongdoing?"

Dog:    "Sure - Every time they come home."

Dr.:    "And what happens?"

Dog:    "They punish us when we run to greet them at the door."

Dr.:    "Perhaps they don't like the exuberant goosing, pawing, licking and jumping-up. Why don't you sit..."

Dog:    "That's a good idea! Never thought of that... But they loved all the attention and physical affection when we were puppies."

Dr.:    "What I meant to say was, why don't you sit down and talk it out with your owners?"

Dog:    "Oh, they never listen. Whenever we sit, they just say "Heel, Sit, Heel, Sit..," and after going round in circles, we come back to where we started. It all seems so pointless."

Dr.:    "Have you tried pleading with your owners?"

Dog:    "All the time. But it's always worse if we act obsequiously. Then they assume we misbehaved on purpose and punish us all the more severely."

Dr :    "Don't you ever get angry?"

Dog:    "If we get angry, they kill us."

Dr.:    "That's terrible! What can I possibly do to help the plight of pet dogs?"

Dog:    "Well for starters, you might consider publishing a Puppy Training Manual for People. "

Dr.:    "Consider it done!"

# The Story of SIRIUS

Sirius, of course, is the dog star - the brightest star in the Heavens. It is in the constellation Canis Major. Also, Sirius is the name of a puppy training program, which I developed in 1980. The SIRIUS program was the very first off-leash, behavior, temperament and home obedience training program designed specifically for puppies.

SIRIUS Puppy Training was actually named after a beagle called Sirius - a puppy of the Seventies. He was a most obnoxious and bellicose puppy. His mother Zelda was a nasty piece of work - she wouldn't even share food with her own offspring. Sirius's early days were a case of 'put-up or shut-up' - a philosophy he extended to his three litter mates - all females who he bullied relentlessly. Understandably, Sirius soon developed an inflated view of his own importance.

One fine day, when Sirius was just 10 weeks old, Zelda and her litter were moved into a large outdoor run along with two older litters and 12 adult dogs. Even though he was a moose-like pup (and grew

*Sirius - a big fish in a small food bowl*

up to be the largest beagle west of the Mississippi), Sirius' station in life changed dramatically - from a big fish in a little pond to a little fish in a big pond. Sirius foolishly attempted to trample the First Bitch Amendment to Canine Hierarchical Law - "I have it and you don't." Sirius tried to take over Mimi's food bowl. Even though she was only a few weeks older than Sirius, Mimi was considerably larger and wiser, and she effectively '-ectomised' his macho. Virtually overnight, Sirius was changed from a growly, macho, pandemonious, big jerk into an obsequious, deferential, wiggly-wormy, big jerk. I was amazed how a relatively simple social manipulation could cause such dramatic changes in a dog's behavior and underlying temperament. Even then, I realized the overwhelming importance of temperament modification for pet dogs.

After leaving Academics, Big Red (my 1965 Mustang) and I drove to all of the 48 continental United States (including Nebraska) and then we returned to California in want of a job. It had to be interesting, worthwhile, involving animals, and above all, it had to be fun. Also, at that time, I had just acquired a Malamute pup - Totemtok's Omaha Beagle. I had phoned just about every dog trainer in Northern California, but no one would take him in classes until he was six months old. *Voila!* SIRIUS Puppy Training! - Classes for Omaha. The concept of off-leash, lure-reward puppy training was not new. (In fact, it was so old that it's new again!) That's how we trained dogs when I was a kid.

SIRIUS Puppy Training classes started at the Oakland SPCA and in 1981 moved to Live Oak Park in Berkeley, California, where they are still held. Currently SIRIUS offers classes at a number of locations throughout Northern California, Hawaii and Manhattan. Also, many other trainers have adopted and individually adapted our techniques, and now, similar classes are held throughout the States and abroad.

*My Dad lure-reward training his*
*Springer Spaniel in the Fifties*

# INTRODUCTION

This manual was originally written as a 'puppy training guide' - an adjunct to SIRIUS Puppy Training classes and to our SIRIUS video for teaching puppies to come, sit, heel, stand, down and stay, i.e., for teaching a new dog old tricks. However, techniques for teaching puppies, which are new to this world, too young to know better and too small to push and pull around, are also ideal for teaching adult dogs, which are new to you and/or new to training. In fact, the principles contained herein also represent the methods of choice for teaching old dogs both new and old tricks, for retraining adult dogs that have become set in their ways or for teaching a well-trained adult dog additional commands. If you also have an older dog at home, by all means start training the old geezer along with the puppy. Lure-reward methods are ideal for small, active breeds that are difficult to guide into position and for enormous sack-of-potato breeds that are virtually impossible to guide or force into position.

Off-leash, lure-reward techniques rarely involve touching the dog until it responds correctly. Consequently, human hands are used primarily for petting and praising the puppydog for getting it right, rather than physically correcting, pushing, pulling and jerking the dog for getting it wrong. Thus, the dog quickly develops a positive feeling about people and about training. For this reason, lure-reward techniques are the method of choice when working with dogs that have existing temperament problems, e.g., fearful and/or aggressive dogs. Approaching and reaching for a shy dog, let alone pushing and pulling it around, tend to make the dog more fearful, causing it to run and hide. Aggressive dogs similarly resent being manhandled and might convince the trainer to run and hide!

It is not coincidental that variations on this training philosophy are used worldwide for training grizzly bears, killer whales, birds of prey, big cats (lions and tigers), collegiate laboratory rats, college students, employees, bosses, children and husbands. Try terrorizing a tiger, pushing and pulling a puma, forcing a lion to sit straight or popping a grizzly bear on leash, and you will soon alter your perspective on training.

Without a doubt, puppyhood is the most crucial period of a dog's life - a time when experiences are new and exert a maximal and long-lasting effect on shaping the dog's future personality. As such, puppyhood is the opportune time to influence the course of behavioral development. It is much, MUCH easier to teach good habits from the outset and prevent personality problems from developing than to attempt to eradicate bad habits.

If the most important time is puppyhood, then the second most important time in a dog's life is right now! Whatever has happened in the past - for better or for worse - is history. If the dog did not have the benefits of early training and socialization as a pup, this is indeed unfortunate, but it is of little use crying over spilt milk. The dog must be trained and socialized NOW! The methods are the same; it will just take longer to accomplish.

*...and for teaching old dogs new tricks!*
*(Ashby's first lesson at eleven years of age)*

Dogs are dogs. And surprising though it may seem to some folk, unless given appropriate instruction and guidance, puppies will grow up to behave like dogs. Moreover, many owners are shocked by the sheer speed of transition from puppyhood to adolescence. In only three or four months, that cute, cuddly and bumbling puppy is transformed into an extremely strong and lively adolescent dog of almost adult proportions.

And without a doubt, an out-of-control adolescent dog is the worst houseguest imaginable. The secret is to start training NOW!

It is unrealistic to expect all dogs to grow up automatically to behave like Lassie. 'Lassie' was, in fact, several highly trained dogs. If you have rules and regulations as to how you would like your dog to behave as an adult, do not keep these rules a secret from the puppy. Otherwise, your dog will predictably break rules it did not know existed and no doubt, will be punished for its inevitable 'transgressions'.

Educate your dog. From the beginning, effectively indicate how you would like your dog to behave and profusely praise it for doing so, before even considering punishing the dog for misbehaving. Understanding a dog as a dog and providing necessary guidance will allow the relationship between dog and owner to develop to the fullest. A well behaved dog with a good temperament is a joy to own. But a perpetual misdemeanant or an ill-tempered dog can be an ongoing nightmare for the dog's family, friends and neighbors, as well as for anyone else who comes into contact with the dog, especially including veterinarians and groomers. However, the nightmare tends to be short-lived, since dogs with behavior and temperament problems generally have short lifespans. Dogs that bite, fight and destroy the home environment are seldom kept around for long. For the dog, a lack of education usually spells disaster. Indeed, even simple and common behavior problems, such as chewing and housesoiling, can be the equivalent of a terminal illness.

Without appropriate human guidance, the puppy will develop a series of potential problems as it matures into an adolescent and adult dog. The problems are no great secret; they are utterly predictable. Expected problems fall into three categories:

1. *Temperament Problems* (aggression - biting people, fear of people, fighting with dogs, fear of dogs, hyperactivity)
2. *Behavior Problems* (housesoiling, chewing, digging, barking and jumping-up)
3. *Obedience Problems* (pulling on-leash, running away and not coming when called)

In reality, all aspects of obedience training may be accomplished at any time in the dog's life. (What a thing to say in a puppy training manual!) It just so happens to be easier and quicker to train the dog as a pup. Similarly, although it can be fun to train a dog of at any age, it's a lot more fun training puppies. However, we should not be seduced by the sight of young pups eagerly responding off-leash to the owner's requests and handsignals, lest we forget obedience training is only the tertiary goal of our puppy training program. Temperament training and behavior modification are much more important concerns.

Behavior problems similarly may be resolved in adulthood, but the older the dog, the harder the prospect. Once problems become fixed as habits, it is necessary to first break the old bad habits before teaching new good ones. It makes so much more sense just to teach good habits from the outset.

Temperament problems, however, MUST be prevented during puppyhood.

## TEMPERAMENT PROBLEMS

Temperament problems must be viewed in a developmental context, and temperament training must be accomplished during puppyhood. To delay is utter folly. Attempting to resolve adult temperament problems, such as biting, fighting and fearfulness, is extremely time-consuming, difficult, often dangerous and usually, well beyond the effort and expertise of the average dog owner. On the other hand, preventive measures are easy, effective, virtually effortless, and even enjoyable. The most important item on the agenda of any puppy training and socialization program must always be temperament training - providing an educational forum for pups to learn social skills and to develop the confidence and social savvy for interaction on a friendly basis with other dogs and people. Preventive intervention is the key.

The temperament of every dog needs to be modified to some degree - molded to suit the owner's particular lifestyle. All dogs are different. Some dogs lack confidence, whereas others are pushy. Some are sluggish, but others are too active. Some are shy and reserved, standoffish, asocial, or antisocial, whereas others are overly friendly and rambunctious.

Socialization and play are essential for a pup to develop the sound temperament and solid disposition necessary for domestic living. Specifically, pups must be allowed to play with other puppies and dogs and to enjoy numerous positive interactions with a wide variety of people, especially children and men.

## Fighting and Fearfulness

Puppy play enables the youngster to learn the appropriate context of individual elements of its behavioral repertoire. An inadequately socialized dog will lack confidence in social interactions, as evidenced by hiding and snapping or by mucho-macho snarling and growling - an unnecessarily stressful way to live.

If owners allow their pups sufficient opportunities to play with other puppies and dogs, most potential dog-dog problems take care of themselves. The pups virtually train themselves to be friendly and outgoing, and a socialized dog would much rather play with other dogs than fight or hide. Puppies do, however, require considerable human guidance to prevent the development of fearfulness and aggressiveness towards people.

## Fear & Aggression towards People

ALL dogs are potential biters, and ALL dogs have to be TRAINED never to bite people. Please, please, please, never forget this. Moreover, if there were ever a case for the mandatory use of food lures and rewards in training, it is for the routine prevention of temperament problems. By enjoyable exposure to a variety of people, especially children, (e.g., in class or in puppy parties), dogs become accustomed to meeting and enjoyably interacting with strangers and children. Dogs that like people are less likely to feel the need to bite them.

Owners must learn how to inhibit biting behavior: firstly, to inhibit the force of biting (until all pressure is eliminated and the pup only mouths gently) and then, secondly, to inhibit the incidence of mouthing. Additionally, owners must desensitize the dog to potentially threatening situations, such as around valued objects, (e.g., food bowl, bones and toys), with strangers and/or children, during friendly (but unwanted) petting and hugging, and during aversive (painful) handling and restraint.

Biting is such a dangerous problem that we employ a three-pronged, multiple-intervention program, emphasizing:
1. inhibiting the force of puppy biting
2. inhibiting the incidence of puppy mouthing/biting
3. desensitizing the dog to every conceivable potential provocation.

The bite-inhibition exercises are vitally important, because unforeseen situations may still arise from time to time, for which we have not adequately proofed and prepared the dog: For example, if a child-Batman jumps on the dog's ribcage or if the dog's tail is shut in a car door. Should the dog attempt to bite in these situations, with good bite-inhibition training, it will inflict minimal damage, if any.

## BEHAVIOR MODIFICATION

Nip behavior problems in the bud. Try to modify the dog's behavior before potential, or incipient, problems become full-blown. In the absence of sufficient instruction (behavior modification), the dog will be left to improvise in its search for amusement. Furthermore, inappropriate expression of these behaviors will become an integral part of the dog's routine, i.e., the behaviors will become habits - bad habits! No doubt owners will deem the dog's improvisations as quite unacceptable and consequently, punish the dog for breaking rules it did not even know existed.

Dogs misbehave for two reasons: because they are just acting like dogs and because owners either allow or unintentionally encourage them to express their basic canine nature in ways which are unacceptable. Many owners do not realize their dog's behavior is a problem. Some may realize the problem but ignore it. Others unintentionally reinforce the dog's problematic behavior, and yet others exacerbate existing problems and cause additional ones under the guise of training. All too often, the 'treatment' is the cause!

Most irritating behavior problems are, in fact, quite normal canine behaviors - an attempt on the part of the dog to adapt to the domestic environment. The dog's behaviors are quite normal *per se*, rather it is their manner of expression which the owner considers inappropriate - either in terms of inappropriate timing, inappropriate placement, or inappropriate object choice. Since the owner has placed the dog in an abnormal environment restricted by walls and fences and deficient in social complexity, and it is the owner (and not the dog) who considers the nature of the dog's behavior unacceptable, then perhaps it should be the owner who provides the dog with appropriate and acceptable alternative outlets for the expression of its basic doggy nature. The owner must at least meet the dog halfway and establish a mutually agreeable contract vis a vis the dog's conduct in urban and rural neighborhoods.

The dog must be taught domestic alternatives for its normal doggy behaviors, i.e., what to chew, where to eliminate, where to dig, when to bark, when to jump-up and when to be hyperactive. For example, by giving the dog a treat each time it eliminates outside, the dog soon learns that it can cash in its urine and feces for food treats only when the owner is present. Consequently, the dog would much rather eliminate in its toilet area when the owner is around, i.e., the dog has joined our team. Occasional mistakes may still occur, but basically, the potential housetraining problem has been decimated.

*The dog must be taught appropriate alternatives for its normal doggy behaviors, e.g., where to eliminate!*

21

# OBEDIENCE TRAINING

Obedience training is necessary for owners to communicate with their dogs - specifically, to control the dogs' body position, location and activity. Some form of functional obedience training is necessary for all dogs, no matter what their station in life.

Training should not be a drag. On the contrary, it can be and indeed, should be a lot of fun for both you and your dog. Rigid, relentless and repetitive drilling, countless corrections and perpetual pushing and pulling all belong to yesteryear - a legacy of the confused few, who foolishly championed might over right and brawn over brain. In fact, if at any time during your dog's education either you or your dog are not having a good time, then you are doing something wrong. Time to change to Plan B! Think of dog training as a game of mixed-doubles in tennis - complex and precise rules, but it's still fun. Certainly, you have to practice and work to improve the game. But above all, it should always be fun.

Neither should training require a lot of time. Of course, the more time you spend, the more you will enjoy living with your dog, and the more your dog will enjoy living with you. But, by profitably employing our supposedly superior cognitive powers, lure-reward training becomes easy, efficient and effective. By successfully integrating training into your daily routine, it is possible to train your dog in the course of everyday living without substantially deviating from your existing lifestyle. Similarly, integrating training into the life of the dog produces a greater reliability and willingness to comply.

People tend to think training involves teaching the dog the meaning of commands. Which it does, but this is only the first step. Effective home-training comprises three stages:
  1. teaching the meaning of words used as instructions
  2. teaching the relevance of complying to these instructions
  3. enforcing the dog's response

The meaning of commands may be taught quickly and easily using lure-reward training techniques. Once the pup has grasped the meaning of our instructions, there is seldom need to enforce the pup's response, because it complies reliably and willingly. Thus, by far the most important phase in training involves teaching the relevance of commands, i.e., teaching the dog to want to comply.

Just because the dog understands the meaning of what we ask does not necessarily mean that it will do what we say. Often the dog fails to comprehend the relevance of our instructions, and occasionally, our instructions are at odds with the dog's wishes. For example if we ask a dog to repeatedly alternate between "Sit" and "Down," an intelligent hound might muse "Make up your mind. Do you want me to sit? Or do you want me to lie down?" Try asking a person to repeatedly stand up and sit down, and see how long the human performs. Dogs are no different. The dog may know what we mean but simply just does not see the point in doing it, especially if it would rather be doing something else, such as sniffing the grass, playing with other dogs or treeing a squirrel. The dog does not want to comply because it views training and fun to be mutually exclusive.

Integrated training is the secret to solving the above problems - numerous, extremely short training sessions using life-rewards. By asking a dog to sit before letting it sniff the grass, run in the park or play with other dogs, it quickly grasps the relevance - the true meaning of the word "sit": "Ahhh! You mean if I sit, you'll take off my leash and let me run in the park." 'Running in the park', 'playing with dogs' and other distractions to training are conveniently converted into rewards, which now may be used to facilitate training. Similarly, have the dog 'sit for its supper', sit before it jumps in your lap, and sit before any remotely enjoyable activity, and these too will become high-level life-rewards. In no time at all, the dog's obedient responses become self-reinforcing, because the dog wants to do what we ask.

The success of dog training lies in proving to the dog that sitting, for example, is a great idea - the dog's idea. In a sense, we are trying to convince the dog that it is training us. The dog's response (sitting) now becomes the dog's 'request' to prompt its owner to respond appropriately by allowing the dog to indulge in its preferred activities. The dog sits, and its owner obediently opens doors and serves supper.

## PET DOG TRAINING

This manual focuses on training true companion dogs. As such, it emphasizes the development of the dog's demeanor and disposition. No amount of obedience training will ever compensate for a tricky temperament. Temperament training and behavior modification are always of paramount importance.

In addition, the selected obedience exercises have a functional and applied 'for-the-home' bias. Whereas many dog training texts and classes only comprise exercises necessary for a dog to compete in obedience trials, this guide primarily describes those exercises which are beneficial, or essential, for living with a dog. For example, we teach off-leash control for the home before we teach on-leash control for the streets. We teach off-leash following and on-leash walking before we teach precision on-leash heeling. We teach 'Settle Down and Shush' (remain quietly in this designated spot in any comfortable body position) before we teach specific sit-stays, stand-stays and down-stays (both prone and supine).

Pet dog training and competition training have different goals, but they are not mutually exclusive. On the contrary, they greatly complement each other. A comprehensive pet dog training program certainly improves confidence and performance reliability for competitive choreography. Remember, the value of a working dog with a dodgy temperament is zero. Similarly, competition training markedly improves precision and pizzazz. I strongly recommend competition work for all dogs - it's a lot of fun.

I have tried my utmost to keep this manual short and to the point, but there is so much to tell. Consequently, I have summarized the major points:

## Start Training Now

First impressions are lasting impressions. It is important to establish the domestic status quo as soon as possible. Don't delay - start training today. Turn to the Training section, and give it a whirl! See how far you and your puppy can progress in just one 10-minute session. Praise yourself and the dog, and then, sit down and read the rest of the manual.

## Puppy Parties for People

First impressions are particularly important for your pup's personality development. Expose and familiarize the puppy to everything it might encounter as an adult - strange situations, loud noises, sudden movements and especially, people. Actively train your dog not just to tolerate the company of family, friends and strangers but also to thoroughly enjoy the company of people, especially children. Dogs are dogs, and when they feel threatened, they may bite. If you do not have children living at home with you, beg and borrow them from relatives, friends, or neighbors, and arrange your first puppy party NOW! All dogs are potential biters. However, dogs which like people seldom feel the need to bite. Socialization is essential, as are the specific handling and gentling, confidence-building and bite-inhibition exercises. It is up to you - the owner - to train your puppy not to bite as an adult.

## Puppy Parties for Pooches

A well socialized dog would much rather play with dogs than hide or fight. It is especially important that your dog gets along with your friends' dogs and your neighbors' dogs. When your pup has completed its full series of puppy shots, arrange a puppy party or a picnic in the park, so these dogs may get acquainted.

## Your pup will soon be an adult dog

Teach your dog appropriate ways to express its basic doggy nature. Otherwise, it will improvise and no doubt, act in a manner that you find inappropriate and annoying. Your dog must be taught where to eliminate, what to chew, where to dig, when and for how long to bark and how to greet people. Bear in mind, there are an infinite number of ways a dog can get things wrong, but only one way to get it right. Consequently, teach the right way from the outset. Establish ground rules now. Always imagine your cute little pupski as a full-grown adult dog, and treat it accordingly.

25

## Practice turning your dog OFF!

Twenty times a day, instruct your pup to 'settle-down and shush'. Practice on-leash at home, and on walks. Establishing an early precedent of numerous 'little-quiet-moments' with your puppy augurs well for a lifetime of enjoyment with the dog as an adult. Otherwise, Rover's rumbustious and rambunctious behavior will batter your brain and destroy your dwelling, and fun-loving Rover's feast of life will depend on Damocles.

## Practice turning your dog ON!

Fifty times a day, request the pup to come and sit for a pet or a pat, a toy or a treat. The secret to producing a reliably obedient dog lies with numerous, extremely short (less than five-second) training sessions each day - many times a day in different locations indoors, in the yard and on walks. Many dogs develop a Jekyll and Hyde type personality; if you have their attention, they will do anything, but if you don't, they won't! Focus on 'Sit' or 'Down' as emergency attention-getting commands.

## 'Sit' is Common Canine Courtesy

From the outset, train your puppy: to sit for its supper, to sit for treats and toys, to sit for pets, pats and praise, to sit to go outside, to sit to come inside, to sit to climb into the owner's lap, etc. Just because you have taught your pup the meaning of the word 'sit' does not mean it will necessarily comply. Requesting the dog to sit before all enjoyable doggy activities adds relevance to the instruction. Once the pup understands "Sit" means: "Please may I...?", the pup will want to sit when requested. Remember, sitting is the simple solution for so many problems.

## 'Sit' to Say Hello

Especially, train your pup to 'sit' for all greetings - at the front door and on the street. It is unfair to encourage and reward a puppy for jumping up, only to punish the dog as an adult for doing the same thing. Later on, a well-trained dog may be allowed to jump-up on cue at the person's convenience and discretion, i.e., "Give us a hug!"

## To Pull or Not to Pull?

Never, NEVER let the puppy pull on leash. Do not let anybody walk the dog until they can walk with a loose leash. Trying to get an adolescent dog to quit a leash-pulling habit is on par with trying to convince a person to give up chocolate or smoking. Later on, at the owner's discretion, the dog may be trained to pull on cue - to help the owner uphill or to power a sled on the snow.

# HOW TO TEACH A NEW DOG OLD TRICKS

# I. TEMPERAMENT TRAINING

## *Requiem for Rover. Act I*

*Rover had been perfectly trustworthy for a number of years until suddenly, out of the blue, he attacked a visiting child without warning and without reason. The next morning, Rover seriously attacked his owner. Many would argue that Rover was making his play to dominate members of the domestic pack. However, Rover was not habitually an aggressive cur but acted perfectly fine the majority of the time and only attacked on two specific occasions. Consequently, he was considered to be unpredictably aggressive. Rover was diagnosed as having idiopathic aggression. And, with the problem neatly labeled, categorized and pigeon-holed, Rover was sentenced and summarily executed.*

## The Owners' Story

Rover was just your normal faithful pooch. The owners were not aware of any signs of aggression. On the contrary, the owners vividly remembered, they never experienced any of the expected mouthing or puppy biting problems when Rover was a youngster. Thinking back, the owners were aware of some situations which made Rover feel uneasy, but they ignored them, thinking they were not that serious. The owners were aware: 1) Rover always took a long while to warm to strangers, 2) Rover was not overly fond of kids, 3) Rover was a mite hand-shy, and 4) Rover was, at times, understandably protective of its food, bones and toys - I mean he was a dog after all!

Rover appeared to be sound and comparatively friendly, at least most of the time. He only appeared to be uneasy and apprehensive in certain specific situations, which were easily predictable and therefore, easy to avoid or ignore. That is, until Rover unexpectedly bit the child.

Mum was shocked, frightened and did not know what to do. She locked Rover in the basement while she took the child to hospital. Both Mum and Dad loved Rover very much. Dad had a soft spot for the dog, and when told of the bite after returning home, he could scarcely believe what had happened. Dad went to the basement. Rover was his normal happy-go-lucky self and showed no signs of remorse. Dad put down his brief case and car keys and severely punished the dog. Rover was confined to the basement overnight, while the owners decided what to do. In the morning, Dad went in to see the dog before leaving for work. At first, Rover seemed a little scared and dejected but responded eagerly and happily to a series of obedience commands: come, sit, lie-down, sit and shake hands. As Dad reached down to pat Rover and say good-bye, he reached in his pocket for his car keys... And Bam! Rover attacked and bit him several times up on the forearm.

The owners felt they could not live with a dog which bit children, and they were extremely perturbed by Rover's vacillatory mood swings and the unpredictability of his aggressive outbursts. Reluctantly, they decided to have Rover euthanized.

## Rover's Story

Rover had a very different story. In cross-examination he maintained: 1) he had repeatedly warned his owners - numerous times over the years leading up to the incident, 2) he warned the child immediately prior to bite, and 3) he had many, MANY reasons for biting.

Ever since puppyhood, Rover had tried to convince his owners: 1) he felt decidedly on-edge when strangers invaded his living space, 2) he felt extremely uneasy and apprehensive  around children, 3) he really did not like people reaching for his neck to grab and jerk his collar and 4) he felt completely at odds when people approached his food bowl (presumably because he had become accustomed to eating alone, intentionally isolated by the owners in some out-of-the-way part of the house).

Rover could not understand why the owners failed to respond to his desperate warnings. Sometimes his warnings were ignored, and other times, they were intentionally suppressed. Indeed, Rover was punished whenever he growled. Rover decided that his owners did not want him to growl, and so the warnings ceased. But the underlying problems were still unresolved - a time bomb, silently ticking away. But certainly, Rover had warned his owners - many times over. And certainly, he had many reasons to be upset. He especially could not comprehend Dad's irrational attack on returning home from work and feared that his owner might have some form of idiopathic human 'rage' syndrome.

## What Really Happened?

1) Rover had never bitten a stranger. He had never even growled at a stranger. However, he never greeted them either. Instead, Rover stayed a respectful distance and would only cautiously investigate strangers after carefully observing them for several minutes. Rover felt uneasy with strangers because he had not been given adequate opportunity to interact with many people. Whereas the average person talks with at least 30 people a day, Rover usually interacted with only three - all family members. Over the past three years, Rover had become progressively desocialized towards people.

2) Rover lived with Mum, Dad and their six-year-old son, Johnny. Rover had never bitten Johnny and maybe never would, but on the other hand, Rover did not particularly like Johnny. The child, the bothersome bane of any dog, relentlessly pursued Rover everywhere - poking, prodding, grabbing, hugging and crawling all over him. Rover was tormented by the child's incessant provocative behavior and warned the child to desist. Worried by the dog's 'intolerance', the parents punished Rover for growling. As Rover quickly learned to associate the parents' unpleasant actions with the child's presence, he became increasingly tense and uneasy. Eventually, he felt threatened by the mere presence of the child. However, when unsupervised, the child continued to seek out and unintentionally harass the dog, and so, Rover took evasive action, doing his utmost to stay out of the child's way.

3) Rover had never snapped or growled when handled by the parents, but he used to duck his head slightly whenever Dad reached for his collar. Also, both Rover's veterinarian and groomer had mentioned Rover had always been quite a handful during routine

examinations, and recently, he had become decidedly difficult to restrain, especially when having his ears cleaned.

4) Rover had never snapped, growled or actively tried to protect his food bowl. But then he never had the opportunity, since he always ate alone, and everybody had been instructed not to go near the dog when he was eating. (While this may be sound advice, it is essential that Rover be instructed how to act in the face of uninvited guests around his food bowl.) Even so, an observant owner might have noticed subtle posturing cues around the food bowl and passive protection with toys and bones. And of course, there was the time when Dad had to chase down Rover and drag him from beneath the bed to forcibly remove a box of masticated paper tissues from his mouth.

The owner's chose to adopt an 'ostrich-approach'; they made elaborate excuses for Rover's insecurity and for his numerous warnings. Each euphemistic explanation was an exercise in understatement and self deception. And then one day, Johnny's latest best friend, Jimmy, came over to play after school. Rover retired to the family room while the two children played with Jimmy's new toy - a remote controlled plastic Plateosaurus which squirted sparks from its jaws. In the course of play, the little green monster bumped into Rover's aluminum food bowl. "Ahhhh! Dinner time," mused Rover. Rover's anticipation for food overcame his antipathy towards kids in the kitchen, and he expectantly trotted towards his bowl, which he reached at the same time as Jimmy was reaching down to retrieve his toy, inadvertently brushing against Rover's ear and collar in the process. Rover bit Jimmy. And the bite broke the skin.

The medical model for the analysis of behavior problems prompts us to search for a single reason to explain the dog's actions - a direct cause and effect. Usually, however, there are many reasons for a dog to bite, or at least, there are many situations and/or specific stimuli which cause a dog to feel uneasy. With a stranger - a child - next to the food bowl reaching for the dog's collar - whereas none of these stimuli alone were adequate provocation for aggression, the combined anxiety of all four proved too much for Rover, and he felt the need to defend himself. Whereas no single stimulus was extreme in itself, occurring together, the compounded stress of a number of subliminal bite-stimuli exceeded the dog's bite-threshold. Whenever the desire to defend exceeds the level of bite inhibition acquired during development, the dog bites. Certainly Rover had reason to bite the child, four reasons in fact. Basically, Rover had a brittle temperament, like a lake with a smooth covering of fresh snow on ice just half-an-inch thick. It's fine until you jump up and down! It's the last straw that breaks the camel's back. I wonder how many parents, siblings or spouses have felt the same way?

The concept of subliminal bite-stimuli is a more productive theoretical model, both for interpreting individual bite incidents and for implementing a preventive intervention program. It is vital to understand there are usually several reasons for a single bite, and our goal should be to desensitize each one in puppyhood.

Rover's second attack is a little more complicated to interpret, because one of the subliminal bite-stimuli was a superstitious cue. Rover reacted badly to the morning reappearance of Dad (the punisher) in the basement (the punishment area) but then perked up when he realized Dad was OK. However, Rover became uneasy when Dad reached to pat Rover, and poor Rover just lost it with the superstitious cue - the jangling keys.

A superstition is created when, by chance, an otherwise neutral and innocuous stimulus precedes either an extremely good or an extremely bad turn of events. For example, if a football coach eats a chicken sandwich before winning the first victory of the season, the coach may make a habit of eating chicken sandwiches before all subsequent games. Negative superstitions are created when a previously innocuous stimulus precedes a devastating event. For example, if someone walks under a ladder and a bucket of bricks falls on his head, the person will most likely avoid walking under ladders in the future.

In Rover's case, the jangling of the keys preceded the first severe physical punishment in his life. Although there was no permanent or logical cause-and-effect relationship between the stimulus (keys) and the sequence of events (punishment), the punishment was so frightening and unpleasant for the dog that a single chance association between the two was all that was necessary to make Rover extremely edgy upon subsequent exposure to the sound of the keys. From Rover's viewpoint, it wasn't worth taking the chance of risking another beating. And so, Rover issued a pre-emptive strike. Rover attacked first!

Just because Rover's behavior appeared to be unpredictable, doesn't mean it was. Rover's attacks were caused by the summation of a series of well-defined and predictable stress-provoking stimuli. Similarly, just because the owners and/or the victims perceived no warnings, doesn't mean Rover gave no warnings. Over and over, Rover had warned his owners he felt uneasy in certain situations, but over and over, the owners chose to ignore the warnings.

Also, even though Rover knew growling was wrong, he most certainly warned Jimmy to back off immediately prior to the bite. It was hardly Rover's fault his quick and subtle warning went unnoticed and unheeded by a six-year-old child who had never been around dogs in his life. Similarly, Rover warned Dad when he came into the basement. The dog really tried to issue fair warning in both cases. However, over the years, the propensity for issuing warnings had been progressively trained out of Rover. He was punished each time he growled. Misguided training cut the fuse even shorter.

Limiting behavior 'therapy' to punishing a dog for growling, generally makes matters worse. Dogs growl when they feel uptight in specific situations. If a dog is punished, it now has two reasons to be uptight: 1) the initial reason - lack of confidence and 2) the owner/handler's inexplicable aggressive outburst, which destroys what little confidence remains. Now, we have a dog which is still upset but no longer warns us. The priorities are back to front. Firstly, one should resolve the underlying temperament problem and desensitize the dog, and then and only then, should one train the dog not to growl.

Rover's first two attacks were severe, because Rover received only limited bite-inhibition training during puppyhood. Since Rover did not bite and mouth his owners willy nilly as a pup (maybe he was a little shy), he never learned that biting was wrong, and neither did he learn to inhibit the force of his jaws when mouthing people. Moreover, since he was a suburban yuppy-puppy (confined by walls and fences), Rover rarely played with other dogs and so, never learned bite inhibition at all!

# PREVENTING DOG BITES

Rover's case is probably an oversimplification. In reality, for each individual dog, there are at least a dozen or so specific stimuli or situations, that give it the heebie-jeebies. We know the things that upset dogs; they are no great secret. The most common anxiety-provoking stimuli include: children, strangers (especially men and children), people wearing or carrying something out of the ordinary (hats, sunglasses, umbrellas, baseball bats etc.), people acting weird, sudden movements and loud noises, being touched on the muzzle, ears, paws and rear end, being restrained (or hugged) and being around food, bones, toys and other valued possessions.

Unless sufficiently proofed and desensitized, many dogs may feel threatened by the mere presence of people, even by people who may have perfectly good intentions. In fact, social behavior problems may be analyzed and explained largely in terms of eye contact, distance/proximity and physical contact.

During routine puppy husbandry, the single most important goal for every owner is to desensitize the dog to each potentially provocative stimulus. Temperament training comprises a two-stage progressive desensitization process, whereby the dog learns not only to tolerate the proximity, contact and actions of people but also, to thoroughly enjoy the company and actions of people, especially including handling and manhandling by children and/or strangers. And why? Because, one day, a child might inadvertently (or intentionally) frighten the dog during play; a veterinarian or groomer might unavoidably hurt the dog during an examination; the owner might accidentally tread on the dog's paw or shut its tail in the car door. It is better to prepare the dog beforehand.

# SOCIALIZATION

Young pups are often viewed as animated furry toys, rather than the nearly full-size, adolescent dogs they will surely be in just a few months time. Often, puppy owners just cannot conceive their cosseted bundle of fluff could ever pose a problem. Owners must remember they are living with a dog - an animal. When dogs are upset they do not call their lawyer or write a letter of complaint.

They growl and bite.

People tend to forget domestic dogs are not fully domesticated until they have been adequately trained and fully socialized. If a dog (of any breed) has only been partially socialized, it is much more dangerous than a wild animal. Wild animals keep their distance from people, whereas partially socialized dogs live with people and therefore, have greater opportunity to bite when spooked, frightened, or hurt.

Lack of socialization is the major reason why dogs become fearful of people, other dogs, other animals, or the environment. And fearfulness is the major reason why dogs act aggressively towards people, dogs and animals. A fearful dog will usually run and hide in an attempt to avoid confrontation with the frightening stimulus. However, when the frightening stimulus is also alive, it may continue to approach and pursue the dog. When threatened in this manner and with retreat prevented (no chance of escape), the dog's last resort is to try and convince the intruder to retreat by snarling, snapping, barking, or biting.

On the other hand, a socialized dog would much rather play than bite or fight. Socialization is the developmental process whereby puppies and adolescent dogs familiarize themselves with their infinitely varied and ever-changing social and physical environment. Puppies must be exposed and desensitized to everything they are ever likely to encounter as adult dogs. The broader a puppy's experience, the better equipped it will be as an adult dog to cope with changes in the environment. Puppy Parties and Puppy Training classes are the name of the game.

Please remember, we are socializing the puppies for the future. Do not be duped by your boisterous, party-animal puppy. Given normal development and socialization, all young puppies (2-4 months) should appear to be overly friendly and inquisitive - approaching everyone and everything. However, behavior and temperament are constantly changing, depending on the stage of development and the nature of socialization. In the course of normal development, puppies start to shy away from strangers by the time they are 4-5 months old. To maintain their acceptance of strangers, adolescent dogs must be continually socialized to strangers. Similarly, although most young pups love children, adolescent and adult dogs predictably become increasing wary and intolerant towards children. To preserve their love of children, adolescent and adult dogs must be continually socialized with children. The dog must continually be taught how to act around children, just as children must be taught how to act around dogs.

Eight months of age is the most common time for a previously well-socialized puppy to suddenly 'spook' to loud or strange noises, weird happenings, sudden movements, strangers and especially, children. Please remember, we socialize puppies, so that we may continue socializing them throughout adolescence and adulthood, especially during the critical adolescent 'spook' period - six months to two years of age.

## HANDLING AND GENTLING

Why should a dog be hand-shy? Many people argue it is breed specific, due to 'bad' breeding or due to abuse as a pup. Certainly, if a dog ducks its head when a stranger reaches to pet or examine the dog, it is usually because the dog feels insecure around strangers. However, rather than limiting diagnostic etiology to how the dog reacts to the hand, it is a little more illuminating to consider what the hand has done to the dog. There is a maxim, "dog behavior doesn't lie." And for example, if a dog flinches when its owner reaches for the collar, it hardly takes the brain of Einstein to realize the owner's hands have been up to no good around the dog's collar. Now, it may have been something as innocuous as the owner taking hold of the dog's collar to snap on the

*Use training treats to teach your dog to stand-stay and enjoy being examined. Your veterinarian will appreciate it.*

leash to terminate a good time in the park, playing and partying with other pups. Or, the owner may have taken the dog's collar to lead it outside or to banish it to the basement for a day in solitary confinement at home alone. More likely though, the owner grabbed the collar to reprimand or punish the dog.

It is silly to make euphemistic excuses for a dog's intractability and/or lack of confidence in lieu of solving the problem. Regardless of the cause of hand-shyness, we know the problem may be resolved via systematic desensitization techniques, and more importantly, we know hand shyness may be prevented easily and effectively, using basic puppy confidence-building exercises.

There are, of course, times when it is necessary to grab the dog, e.g., if the dog has slipped its collar or about to dash out of the front door. Similarly, at one time or another, a child will probably grab the dog to give it a hug and a squeeze. Consequently, every dog must be proofed to both tolerate and to thoroughly enjoy necessary but unintentionally frightening and possibly painful, grabbing, handling and restraint.

Before the pup's mealtime, take a handful of dried kibble out of its bowl, and give a piece to your pup. Step back, and give another when the pup approaches. Give a third after gently reaching and scratching the pup behind the ear. The next time, reach a little quicker, but still scratch or stroke the pup gently before giving the treat. On subsequent trials, gradually and progressively increase the speed that the hand moves before petting the dog, until it is possible to grab the dog quickly but gently. Then, reach for the dog slowly, carefully take it by the scruff or collar and gently tug before giving the treat. Over the next couple of trials, progressively increase the force of the grasp. In no time at all, it will be possible to grab and vigorously shake the dog by its scruff, and the dog says, "Great! Where's my treat?"

Have family and friends practice this exercise with your puppy. Once the pup has confidence in being handled, it will be less likely to react adversely when grabbed in an emergency. Indeed, potentially frightening handling and manhandling becomes enjoyable roughhousing. The dog learns to associate human hands with petting and giving treats, rather than with physical restraint and punishment.

# BITE-INHIBITION

Puppies bite, and thank goodness they do! Puppy biting is a normal, natural and necessary puppy behavior. In fact, it is puppies who do not mouth and bite as youngsters which augur ill for the future. Puppy play-biting is the means by which dogs develop bite-inhibition, which is absolutely essential later in life.

The combination of weak jaws, extremely sharp needle-like teeth and the puppy penchant for biting results in numerous play-bites, which although painful, seldom cause serious harm. Thus, the developing pup receives essential feedback regarding the force of its bites before it develops strong jaws, which could inflict considerable injury. The greater the pup's opportunity to play-bite with people, other dogs and other animals, the better the dog's bite-inhibition as an adult. For puppies which do not grow up with the benefit of regular and frequent interaction with other dogs and other animals, the responsibility of teaching bite-inhibition lies with the owner.

Certainly, puppy biting behavior must eventually be eliminated. We cannot have an adult dog playfully mauling family, friends or strangers, in the manner of a young puppy. However, puppy biting behavior should not be completely eradicated all at once, otherwise the dog will not learn to inhibit the force of its bite. Instead, puppy biting should be gradually and progressively eliminated via a systematic four-step process. With some dogs, it is easy to teach the four phases in sequence, but with others, puppy biting may be so severe the owners will need to embark on all four stages at once. However, it is always essential the pup first learns to inhibit the force of its bites before biting frequency is eliminated altogether.

## 1. Inhibiting the Force of Bites

*No Painful Bites:* The first item on the agenda is to stop the puppy from hurting people. It is not necessary to reprimand the pup, and certainly, physical punishments are contra-indicated, since they generally make matters worse. Physical punishments and restraint tend to 1) make some pups more excited and 2) damage the puppy's temperament by insidiously eroding its trust in the owner. However, it is essential to let the pup know when biting hurts. A simple "Ouch!"

is usually sufficient. The volume of the 'ouch' should vary according to the dog's mental make-up; a fairly soft 'ouch' will suffice for sensitive critters, but a loud 'OUCH!!!' may be necessary for a wild and woolly beast.

During initial training, even shouting may make the pup more excited, as do physical punishment, restraint or trying to force the pup into confinement. An extremely effective technique with a boisterous puppy is to call the pup a "Jerk!" and then leave the room and shut the door. Allow the pup just one or two minutes 'time-out' to reflect on the loss of its favorite human playmate, and then, return to make up. It is important to indicate you still love the pup; it is the painful bites which are objectionable. Instruct the pup to come and sit, and then, resume playing once more. Ideally, the pup should have been taught not to hurt people well before it is three months old.

It is infinitely preferable to leave the pup in isolation rather than trying to physically restrain the critter and forcibly remove it to a confinement area at a time when it is already out of control. (Of course, this means you should make a point of playing with your pup in an area where it would be safe to leave it unattended should its behavior get out of hand, i.e., in the pup's long-term confinement area.)

The above technique is remarkably effective with lead-headed dogs. This is fortuitous, because trying to physically punish puppies of some Terrier and Working breeds is on par with reprimanding a bowling ball. Physically, they are so tough, but luckily their brains are extremely sensitive; they have sweet dispositions and love to play. Consequently, they just cannot stand to lose a playmate. This is precisely the same way puppies learn to inhibit the force of their bites when playing with each other. If one pup bites another too hard, the bitee yelps, and play is suspended whilst the injured party licks its wounds. The biter learns that hard bites curtail an otherwise enjoyable play session. Hence, the biter learns to bite more softly when the play session resumes.

*No Jaw Pressure At All:* The second stage of training involves eliminating bite-pressure entirely. Even though the 'bites' no longer hurt, when the puppy is munching away, wait for a nibble which is harder than the rest and respond as if it really hurt (even though it didn't). "Ouch, you worm! Gennntly! That hurt me you bully!" The dog begins to think, "Good Lord! These humans are really namby-pamby; I can bite the cat harder than that! These humans are sooooo sensitive. I'll have to be really careful when mouthing their delicate skin." And that is precisely what we want the dog to think - to be extremely careful when playing with people. Ideally, the puppy should no longer be exerting any pressure when mouthing by the time it is 4-5 months old.

## 2. Inhibiting the Incidence of Mouthing

*Always To Stop Mouthing when Requested:* Once your puppy has been taught to mouth gently rather than bite, it is time to reduce the frequency of mouthing by teaching the pup that mouthing is OK until requested to stop. Why? Because it is inconvenient to try to drink a cup of coffee or to answer the telephone with 50 pounds of pup dangling from your wrist, that's why.

Hand-feeding a portion of your pup's supper is a wonderful way to teach the puppy "Off!" and "Take it!" In addition, regular hand-feeding helps preserve the pup's soft mouth and increases the pup's confidence with people around its food bowl. Once the pup has been taught "Off!" with food, the instruction may be used to stop the puppy mouthing. While the pup is mouthing gently, say "Off!" and offer a food treat. Praise the pup when it lets go to take the treat. Remember, the essence of this exercise is to practice stopping the dog from mouthing, and so, each time the pup obediently ceases and desists, allow it to resume mouthing once more. Stop and start the mouthing many times over in a single session. Also, since the puppy really wants to mouth, the best reward for stopping is allowing it to mouth again. When you decide to stop the mouthing session altogether, say "Off!," call the pup to the kitchen, tell it to "Settle Down" and give it a stuffed chewtoy to occupy its jaws.

If ever the pup refuses to release your hand when requested, yelp "OFF!," rapidly extricate your hand from its mouth, storm out of the room mumbling "Right JERK! That's done it! You've ruined it! Finish! Over! No more!" and shut the door in the dog's face. Give the pup a couple of minutes on its own, and then go back and call the pup to come and sit to make up. But no more mouthing for at least a couple of hours.

*Never to Start Mouthing Unless Requested:* By the time your pup is 5 months old, it should have a mouth as soft as a 14 year-old working Labrador. It should never exert any pressure when mouthing, and the dog should immediately stop mouthing when requested to do so by any family member. As discussed earlier, unsolicited mouthing is essential for puppies and acceptable for young adolescents, but it is utterly inappropriate for older adolescents and adult dogs. It would be disastrous for a six-month-old dog to approach a child in the park and commence mouthing her arm, no matter how gentle the mouthing nor how friendly and playful the dog's intentions. This is the sort of situation which gives parents the heebie-jeebies and frightens the living daylights out of the mouthee. At five months of age, at the very latest, the dog should be taught never to touch any person's body or clothing with its jaws unless requested to do so.

Whether or not the dog will ever be requested to mouth people depends on the individual owner. For hapless owners, I recommend they teach the dog to discontinue mouthing people altogether by the time it is 6 months old. Owners who have the mental largesse of a Q-tip quickly let play-mouthing get out of control, which is why many dog training texts strongly advise against games such as play-fighting. However, it is essential to continue bite inhibition exercises, otherwise the dog's bite will begin to drift and become harder and harder as the dog grows older. For such people, I recommend that they regularly hand feed the dog and clean its teeth daily, i.e., exercises which involve a human hand in the dog's mouth. Also, one hopes the dog will have adequate opportunity to maintain bite inhibition by playing with other dogs and animals.

On the other hand, for owners who have a healthy complement of common sense, there is no better way to maintain the dog's soft mouth than by play-fighting with the dog on a regular basis. However, to prevent the dog from getting out of control and to fully realize the many benefits of play-fighting, the owner must play by the rules, and they must teach the dog to play by the rules. (Play-fighting rules are described in detail in our Preventing Aggression Behavior Booklet.)

Play-fighting teaches the dog to mouth hands only (hands are extremely sensitive to pressure) and never clothing. Since shoelaces, ties, trousers and hair have no neurons and cannot feel, the owner cannot provide the necessary feedback that the dog is mouthing too hard, too close to human flesh. Obviously, NEVER put on gloves to play with the dog. This will train the pup to bite much harder than usual! Play-fighting exercises teach the pup that it must adhere to rules regarding its jaws, regardless of how worked-up it may be. Basically, play-fighting teaches the owner to practice controlling the dog at times when it is excited. It is important to refine such control in a structured setting before real-life situations occur.

In addition, play-fighting quickly becomes play-training. Starting each game with a training prelude  with the dog under control (in a down stay for example) produces utterly solid stays at a time when the dog is excited in vibrant anticipation for the game. Similarly, frequently stopping play-fighting for short periods and integrating multiple training interludes (especially heel work and recalls) into the game motivates the dog for eager and speedy responses. Remember, each time you stop the game, you may use the resumption of play as a reward for bonza obedience.

## Potential Problems

*a) Inhibiting Incidence Before Force:* A common mistake is to punish the pup in an attempt to get it to stop biting altogether. At the best, the puppy no longer mouths those family members who can effectively punish the dog, but instead, the pup directs its mouthing sprees towards those family members who cannot control the dog, e.g., children. To worsen matters, parents are often completely unaware of the child's plight, because the pup does not mouth them. At the worst, the puppy no longer mouths people at all. Hence, its education about the force of its bites stops right there. All is fine until someone accidentally treads on the dog's tail, whereupon the dog bites, and in the absence of bite-inhibition, the bite punctures the skin.

*b) Puppies Which Don't Bite:* Shy dogs seldom socialize or play with other dogs or unfamiliar people. Hence, they do not play-bite, and hence, they learn nothing about the power of their jaws. A classic case history comprises a dog which never mouthed or bit as a pup and never bit anyone as an adult, that is until an unfamiliar child tripped and fell on the dog whilst it was gnawing a bone. Not only did the dog bite, but the first bite of the dog's career left deep puncture wounds, because the dog had no bite-inhibition whatsoever. With shy puppies, socialization is of paramount importance, and time is of the essence. The puppy must be socialized immediately, so that it commences playing (and hence biting) before it is 18 weeks old.

Some breeds have a high degree of fidelity towards their owners and consequently, tend to be fairly stand-offish with other dogs and/or human strangers. Some restrict mouthing and biting to family members, and some simply do not mouth at all. Hence, they never learn to inhibit the force of their jaws. Similarly, other breeds, especially some gun dogs and retrievers, have extremely soft mouths as puppies and consequently, never receive any feedback that jaws can hurt. If a puppy does not frequently mouth and bite and occasionally bite hard, it is an emergency. The puppy must learn its limits. And it can only learn its limits by exceeding them during development and receiving appropriate feedback. Plentiful play with other dogs will create a mouthing habit and provide the necessary feedback.

## PROTECTIVENESS

Why should a dog feel the need to protect its bones, toys and food bowl? Are there really owners out there secretly meeting in coffee shops to plot stealing the dog's food and possessions? Then why should people have problems around the dog's food bowl? Because dogs are dogs! It would be unheard of for one dog to ask another, "May I borrow half a cup of kibble? I'll bring it back tomorrow." "Yeah of course you will - when Malamutes miaow!" If dogs only knew people did not want to steal their valued possessions, there would be no need for protection. The solution, then, is for owners to make this quite clear to their dogs, because there will be occasions when it is necessary to temporarily remove food or a valued possession from the dog's jaws. And there will be occasions when a child, a dog and a bone all come together in the same place at the same time.

Many dog owners make the mistake of habitually giving the dog its dinner and then retiring to allow the dog to eat in peace. People, especially children, are additionally warned not to approach the dog while it is eating. While this may be sound and necessary advice, it is not sufficient to prevent the development of protective aggression. On the contrary, isolating a dining dog fosters protectiveness. When a puppy grows up eating alone, it becomes accustomed to solitary supper arrangements. Consequently, it is not surprising that the dog may react adversely when disturbed, especially when rudely startled or painfully interrupted by children. The dog must be actively taught not only to tolerate the proximity and actions of people at feeding time, especially children and strangers, but also to eagerly anticipate and welcome the presence of people around its food bowl.

Sitting with your pup while it eats its first few meals at home establishes a firm foundation of mutual trust, which will last for many years to come. If you hold the bowl and dish out kibble by hand, your puppy will quickly form a positive association with your presence around its food bowl. Moreover, providing company at feeding time affords an ideal opportunity to perform routine handling and gentling exercises whilst your pup is eating.

Sit with your pup while it is eating dry kibble from its bowl, and periodically, put in a hand with a chunk of chicken and give it to the pup. Your puppy will think, "I was certain I checked this bowl for meat. Not a scrap! Then how come this human keeps finding pieces of poultry? No idea! But I hope they stick around!"

Installment feeding, or providing dinner in several courses, is a valuable ploy to get your puppy to re-evaluate its feelings regarding people approaching its food bowl. Weigh your pup's dinner, put it in a bowl on the counter and then, put the pup's empty bowl on the floor and wait. The pup will sniff its bowl and exclaim, "Hey! This is empty! Get over here with some food." By playing the delinquent-waiter routine, your pup now wants you to approach its bowl. Take one piece of kibble, and drop it in the bowl. Retreat and wait for the pup to beg you to approach again. Repeat this half a dozen times. After several small 'starters', drop in a handful of kibble with one hand, and offer a tasty treat with the other. Back up a step, and then, immediately approach to offer another tasty treat while the pup is still

45

eating kibble. Repeat this over and over, and your pup will soon learn human approach and proximity means 'dinner gets better', whereupon the pup will eagerly anticipate occasional human companionship while eating from its food bowl.

At some time in the meal, when your puppy has half consumed its dry food, say "Thank you," take away the bowl and put in a few dollops of juicy, canned food. "Ahh! That's why they wanted the bowl - to give me dessert!" Once your pup is perfectly at ease with family members around its bowl, it is time to work with other people. Divide your puppy's dinner into several courses and have visitors serve your pup with an intentional delay before each course, as in the slow-waiter routine. Not only will the pup tolerate a stranger's presence around its food bowl, not only will the pup actively want the visitor to approach its bowl, but also the pup will want the stranger to hurry up about it. It's as if the puppy muses, "What on earth is that person doing? Hurry up, and get over here with my next course."

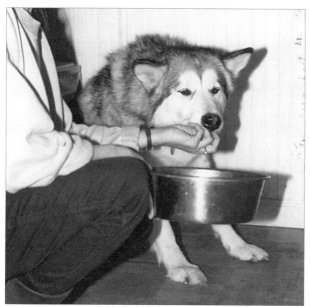

*Hand feed your dog the occasional special treat*
*and it will welcome company at dinner time*

Similarly, build up your puppy's confidence with regards to people around other valued objects. Practice "Off!," "Take it!" and "Thank you!" with less valuable items, and then, work with the pup's bones and chewtoys. Show the pup a bone or chewtoy, and request "Off!" After a while, say "Take it," and let the puppy chew for a while. Then say "Thank you," offer a juicy piece of steak with one hand and take the pup's bone/toy with the other. When the pup has swallowed the steak, give the bone back to the pup. Repeat this a number of times... "Humans are weird. They have numerous tasty treats and masses of meat which they give away. Too generous! They hold one's bone whilst one masticates the meat. Too courteous! And then they give the bone back! Too much! Humans wouldn't make good dogs. Boy, I love humans!"

When performing these exercises with children, first teach your puppy to enjoy the child's company. Sit with the pup while it is eating, and have the child repeatedly enter and leave the room. Praise the pup, and proffer tasty treats when the child is present, but ignore the pup when the child is absent. Once the puppy welcomes the child's presence and associates the child with good times and good treats, the child may offer treats to the pup. At first, put the puppy's food bowl away, and have the child call the pup and offer it a treat from the palm of the hand. Once the child can successfully entice the puppy to come, sit and lie down, the child may perform the food bowl exercises under vigilant supervision. Initially, have the child call the puppy away from its food bowl containing dry kibble to give the pup a delightfully delicious treat, such as turkey, steak, or freeze-dried liver. Have the child instruct the pup to sit before giving the treat. Once the pup quickly and happily leaves its bowl and sits voluntarily in front of the child to receive a treat, the child may be allowed, under strict supervision, to approach the pup to give the treat. Via these exercises, your puppy will soon learn that the child's presence, approach, proximity and contact invariably herald an improvement in dinner quality.

If there were ever a time to use food treats in training, it is to give your puppy a treat when it is chewing on a chewtoy or bone, or eating from its bowl. This changes your pup's entire perspective on people. Your puppy will learn human hands are not coming to take; they are coming to give. And children's hands give the best of all. Indeed, when working with children pull out all the stops - use turkey, lamb, freeze-dried liver - anything that works. Whenever you have a tasty leftover or a bona fide doggy-bag, save it in the fridge for a child to give to your puppy when it is eating supper or busying itself with a chewtoy. In addition, have children feed the pup on a regular basis (always under supervision). In no time at all, your puppy will happily anticipate the presence and presents of children.

## PUPPY PARTIES FOR PEOPLE

Off-leash Puppy Training classes and Puppy Parties are the quickest and most enjoyable way to introduce your young pup to a wide variety of people in a safe and structured setting. Socialization parties effectively proof the puppy to the extent that nothing in real life could possibly be as strange as what has become the boring status quo during Puppy Class.

When Puppy Parties are held before your pup has completed its full series of puppy shots, make sure guests maintain routine hygiene

*It's party time during the Instructor's Workshop at Sirius Puppy Training*

(leaving outdoor shoes outdoors and washing hands before handling the pup). Have a puppy party once or twice a week to invite family, friends and neighbors to meet your puppy. Remember, it is unfriendly neighbors who report barking dogs, and it is usually the neighbors' children who torment dogs causing them to bark in the first place. Although the primary reason for this exercise is for your puppy to meet strangers and children, it also allows neighborhood families to get to know your pup. People are less likely to report a friend's dog for barking, and children are less likely to provoke a pet they know and like.

Weigh out your pup's dinner and divide the dry kibble into separate plastic baggies to be given to each guest to use as lures and rewards when training the pup. This evening, your puppy will be handfed dindins from strangers. Have the strangers take turns in offering a treat. The pup gets the first treat for free: "Hello Pupski! I'm a stranger and here's a treat!" We call this the 'Casablanca Routine' - "This could be the beginning of a beautiful friendship!" However, your pup has to come and sit for the second treat from each person and then, come, sit and lie down for the third. Instruct your friends how to use food lures and rewards to train the pup. After a few treats, your pup will begin to sit automatically when a stranger approaches. Not a bad way to greet a stranger. Sure beats jumping-up. And it sure beats getting beaten for jumping-up.

Strangers may also play Pass the Pup, or Ersatz Veterinarian at the party. The pup is passed from person to person. Each person gives the pup a Casablanca treat, and then looks in one ear and gives a second treat, looks in the other ear and gives a third treat, looks in the pup's mouth and gives a fourth, examines the pup's paws and gives a fifth, and then feels its rear end and gives yet another treat before passing the pup to the next person.

In subsequent Puppy Parties, you might encourage your friends to come dressed in costume, to wear unusual clothes, to carry unusual objects and perhaps to act a little strange. (Or perhaps your friends do this anyway.) Your pup is repeatedly rewarded for partying with these weird and wonderful people. In no time at all, strangers become acquaintances and eventually, good friends. The pup has learned not only to tolerate strangers but also to enjoy and look forward to visits and handling by weirdos. This puts the pup in good stead for visits to parks and for handling by normal people in veterinary clinics, grooming parlors and dog shows. In fact, it is extremely unlikely the dog will ever encounter a real-life situation as peculiar as its early Puppy Parties.

Treats are important when socializing your puppy with strangers. Just because your puppy loves you, doesn't mean to say it will necessarily take to other people. Similarly, your pup may not enjoy praise and petting from people it doesn't know. In fact, many dogs find praise and petting from strangers to be mildly stressful, irritating or downright frightening. On the other hand, treats are useful as lures to entice a puppy to approach a stranger, and once the dog takes a treat as a reward, it will tend to view the stranger in a more favorable light.

Treats are especially effective for men to use as rewards in training, since when rewarding a young puppy, most men sound like Billy Goat Gruff with hemorrhoids. Nothing like a food reward. Similarly, food lures and rewards enable children to successfully control dogs. It is important to encourage children to come to puppy parties for the same reasons we urge the whole family to attend training classes: to educate the children and to educate the pups.

## Educating Children

Every family member must learn to control the dog including children. Using lure/reward training techniques, even four- and five-year-olds can successfully manage all breeds of dog, whether small and fast or large and strong. Whereas puppies and children are a delightful combination, adult dogs and children often have problems. Dog owners may avert tragedy with a simple rule:

No one (i.e., NO ONE) is allowed to interact and/or play with the puppydog without first asking the dog whether it would like to play.

Prospective playmates may ask the puppy to come and sit. If the pup approaches and sits, the person may elect to play. However, if the pup neither comes nor sits, on no account should the person be permitted to play with the puppy. This person has no control over the puppy and will quickly teach the pup many bad habits for which it will no doubt later be punished. This is not fair for your pup, and it is not fair for you the owner.

*The above rule applies to adults as well as children and to men as well as women. A major goal of family pet training is to teach all family members, friends, visitors and strangers, how to control the pup. Untrained people, especially children and adult male friends and family, can ruin a good puppy in no time at all.

## Educating Pups

For dogs growing up with children, parents are well aware it is a full-time task training the children how to act around the puppy and training the pup how to act around the children. A more difficult endeavor, however, is to train a dog how to act around children, when there are no children for practice. Many puppies are owned by people who do not have children living at home. Whereas this may offer a wonderful and peaceful existence for some adult dogs and their owners, it is developmentally disastrous for a puppy. A pup growing up without regular enjoyable contact with children seldom becomes equipped to deal with even routine encounters, let alone possible unpleasant and stressful interactions with children. Generally, everything children do - the screaming, screeching, hugging, pulling, poking, running and falling over -

*Jamie mesmerizing Toby (or vice versa?)*
*during the filming of their television pilot "Sundogs"*

either excites or incites dogs. Just as it is important for all children to learn how to react around dogs, it is important for all dogs to learn how to act around children. And what better time to learn than in puppyhood?

If there are no children in your household, beg and borrow some NOW to perform these simple but crucially important exercises with your puppy. It would be silly to wait until your pup is even 4 months old and completely and utterly foolish to wait until it is 5 months old. Time is of the essence. Potential aggression problems MUST be solved before they develop. Certainly, untrained children can sometimes be a pain. But all the more reason to introduce this 'pain' to your puppy early on, to see how it reacts.

When providing bags of kibble to party guests, make certain the children's bags contain more sought-after appetizers, such as dried

kibble garnished with powdered freeze-dried liver, individual pieces of cheese and meat scraps. Have each child approach to within a couple of yards of the pup and toss a treat on the floor. If your puppy reaches for the treat, instruct the child to back up and offer another treat from the palm of the hand. Thus, your pup's first interaction with a child is; "I'm a child, and here's a treat." First meetings are very important, since they create a deep and long-lasting impression. Once the children have all given a couple of treats, have each child walk right up to

*The Omega Rollover - good for control and good to examine your dog's undercarriage*

52

the pup to offer another. Then, have each child approach and pet the pup whilst giving a treat.

Now, teach the children how to lure the puppy to sit. Most pups sit instantaneously, because they have become familiar with the incorporation of food lures and rewards in training when learning hand-signals. Some pups may sit automatically when they see a child approach. What a lovely way to greet a child, or anyone for that matter. And of course, if the dog sits, it does not jump-up.

This is a wonderful state of affairs for all concerned. Kids feel great, because they can control the pup - marvelous fodder for the children's self-esteem. Not too bad for parental self-esteem either. Indeed, onlooking parents become utterly impressed by their children's embryonic training skills. Owners are secretly relieved their soon-to-be adolescent dog is congenial and compliant with children. And the pups are ecstatic because at long last they have discovered that 'sitting' is the secret command for training children to stand still and deliver treats on cue!

If a dog comes and sits when requested by a child, we know a number of things. Firstly, the dog enjoys the child's company, since it wants to be close; secondly, the child can control the dog using brain instead of brawn; thirdly, the dog has learned to be controlled by children, i.e., if the dog comes and sits when requested, the dog is demonstrating compliance - friendly compliance.

## Omega Rollover

Teach children how to teach your puppy to rollover on its side or back by using the "Bang" command, i.e., rollover-stay in lateral, or supine recumbency. Once the pup is on its back, the child may offer a treat and/or a belly rub or scratch the side of his doodads. In response to the latter, most dogs will raise a hind leg to expose the inguinal area, i.e., the dog performs the quintessential gesture of total doggy-deference. Now we have a unique situation: a two-year-old child may prompt an 80-pound adult dog to demonstrate absolute active appeasement. Moreover, the dog is happily and willingly compliant. And quite frankly, there is no better way for the dog to show compliance to anyone, let alone a child.

53

## PUPPY PARTIES FOR POOCHES

As soon as your pup has completed its full series of puppy shots, it is high time to enroll in an off-leash puppy socialization and training class. Classes provide a formalized forum: 1) for puppies to enjoyably interact and play with a wide variety of people, 2) for owners to learn how to control and obedience train their dogs during distractions, and 3) for puppies to socialize and play with other pups. If given ample opportunity to play as a puppy, during adulthood, most dogs would much rather play with other dogs than hide or fight.

During puppy play sessions, potential or incipient puppy-puppy social problems are resolved before your very eyes. Fearful and/or bellicose pups begin to play with other puppies after only one or two sessions. However, similar social problems in a 5-6 month-old adolescent dog would take several months to resolve. And a shy, standoffish and/or argumentative dog at six months or older may take up to one or two years for rehabilitation. Again, time is of the essence. Get that pup into classes right away! Call the Association of Pet Dog Trainers (1 (800) PET-DOGS) for a list of puppy classes in your area.

If there are no off-leash puppy training and socialization classes in your area, arrange your own. Obtain a list of other puppy owners from your veterinarian, and invite the pups to attend a puppy play group, during your regular People Puppy Parties. Or even better, meet at a different puppy's home each week. A little enjoyable effort now will prevent horrendous potential problems later on.

Off-leash puppy play (play-fighting and play-biting) enables puppies to develop reliable bite-inhibition. Certainly, even well-socialized adult dogs will have occasional disagreements once in a while. In this respect they are not much different from people. There are very few people who can honestly say they have never had an argument, never lost their temper and never physically grabbed another person in anger (usually a sibling, spouse, or child). On the other hand, very few people have seriously harmed or killed anyone. Whereas it is absolutely unrealistic to expect dogs (especially male dogs) never to squabble, it is absolutely realistic to expect dogs to know how to resolve their differences without ripping adversaries limb from limb, in fact, without even drawing blood. Bite inhibition again!

The primary reason for puppy play is for the growing dog to learn to inhibit the force of its bite, before its jaws develop the power to inflict serious damage. Furthermore, these social skills MUST be acquired early in puppyhood. If the adult dog has reliable bite-inhibition, adult fighting problems may be easily and safely resolved simply by letting the adult dogs 'work things out'. However, if the dog does not have good bite-inhibition and harms other dogs, such an approach would be sheer folly. Instead, resolution of the problem will be time-consuming and potentially dangerous. The adult dog must be re-socialized to solve the problem, but it will have to be muzzled so that it may be safely socialized.

# HOW TO TEACH A NEW DOG OLD TRICKS

# II. BEHAVIOR MODIFICATION

## *Requiem for Rover. Act II.*

*Rover crazily jumped all over the kids, knocking them down whenever they visited him in the basement. The parents had always experienced great difficulty catching Rover to confine him, and once he even growled when being forced back into the basement. The parents tried to find Rover a new owner - someone who had more space at home and more time to care for a dog - perhaps an elderly couple on a ranch in Sonoma County.*

*In reality, the likelihood Rover would live out his life with some loving couple on some mythical ranch in Sonoma was slim indeed. Instead, Rover was given the opportunity to find a new owner at the local humane society. However, Rover's chances for the grand prize - a loving, caring owner - were similarly slim. There were just so many unwanted dogs, and in the humane society lotto of life, more than 80% of dogs are euthanized. Rover's chances of euthanasia were even greater because he was uneducated, unruly and uncontrollable; he was not housetrained, and he had bad chewing, digging and barking habits. Finally Rover found his ranch; he found desperate peace in that big ranch in the sky. And why?*

Rover's sad and predictable fate reflects the fate of millions of other dogs. Less than half of domestic dogs get to celebrate their first birthday. In fact in the United States, humane societies alone have to euthanize approximately 20 million pets each year! Thus one pet dies every 1.6 seconds. The sheer enormity of this problem raises a number of questions about Rover's short-lived life:

*Why was Rover confined to the basement in the first place?*
Presumably, because he couldn't be left in the yard, since he excavated indiscriminately, and the neighbors complained about his incessant barking. Of course, excessive digging and barking are in

themselves indicative that the dog has been left outside and unattended for long periods of time.

*But why was Rover isolated outdoors?*
Presumably, because he couldn't be trusted when left unattended indoors. Because the dog would watch racy movies on the telly? No. Simply because the dog would indiscriminately chew and soil the house when left indoors. So, what we really have here is a simple housesoiling problem.

*Why was Rover not housetrained?*
Because the owner had the mental wherewithal of a dewdrop? Not necessarily. Presumably, the owner was unaware how easy it is to housetrain a dog. Information is the key. Let's get this dog housetrained, so that it may be successfully re-integrated into household living once more.

Basically, a simple housetraining problem precipitated a vicious circle of events. At each step, Rover was progressively isolated and confined for longer periods, and at each step, more problems developed. A dog improvises in its choice of chewtoys and toilet because it has received insufficient instruction regarding the owner's choice of chewtoys and toilet areas. A dog confined to the backyard will not magically housetrain itself. Rather it will become an indiscriminate chewer and eliminator. And, if left unattended outdoors for long periods of time, it will also become an indiscriminate digger and an excessive barker. This was true for poor Rover. Understandably, the neighbors complained, and he was further isolated and confined to the basement, which, with his many bad habits acquired from neglect, he proceeded to haphazardly, but effectively, destroy.

The dog is a highly social animal. Isolation from the rest of the household drastically increases the dog's yearning to socialize and increases the dog's excitement when it sees family members. Consequently, the dog becomes uncontrollably rambunctious whenever allowed inside, and eventually, it is no longer allowed inside. Of course, the poor dog will go crazy with joy should anybody deign to venture outdoors. This was Rover's problem: He was simply too happy to see his owners.

# A Dog's a Dog

Facing up to simple behavior problems and solving them is a much more productive philosophy. Confinement and social isolation are not permanent solutions. I have always thought that if a person wants something to confine in the yard and tie to a tree, why not get another tree? Tie the two together with a hammock, relax and read a book on dog training. Then get on, and train the dog. Train the dog where to eliminate, what to chew, where to dig, when to bark and how to greet people. It's really very easy.

Certainly, until the puppy knows the house rules, we have to keep it out of mischief - temporarily confined to a single room or to an outdoor run. But once the dog has been taught the rules of the house and garden, it may be allowed to have full run of the house and garden. Confinement is a temporary necessity until the dog can be trusted in the house. Confinement is not a permanent solution.

Owners must acknowledge a dog is a dog, and it will need to do doggy things. Chewing, digging, barking, eliminating and greeting owners are all normal, natural and necessary canine behaviors. It is folly to try to prevent a dog from ever acting like a dog. It is unfair, inhumane and quite impossible to try to stop a dog from barking, chewing, digging and eliminating altogether. This would be as silly as trying to prevent a dog from wagging its tail or burying a bone. And it would be as successful as trying to cork an erupting volcano.

Punishment-oriented training methods are relatively inefficient and ineffective, tending to cause more problems than they actually resolve. However, it appears to be human nature in most relationships to ignore all that is good and to moan and groan at the bad. Rather than teaching a dog what we want it to do, we tend to punish the dog for making mistakes, i.e., for breaking rules it didn't even know existed. So-called 'training' is all but limited to punishing the dog each time it misbehaves. Unfortunately, punishment-training is only effective if the dog is punished each and every time it misbehaves. If the dog is allowed to 'get away with it' just once, the entire lesson breaks down. Indeed, rather than learning the inappropriateness of its behavior in the domestic setting, the dog learns that it is unwise to behave in that manner when the owner is present. Thus the dog begins to associate punishment with its owner - just one of the many pitfalls of punishment-training. But it gets worse.

Since a dog must act like a dog, but it is understandably reticent to risk wanton wrath by 'misbehaving' when the owner is present, the dog's only alternative is to misbehave when the owner is absent, i.e., the owner has created an owner-absent behavior problem. Many misguided owners like to think that owner-absent problems are the result of separation anxiety. Quite the contrary, the etiology is more likely separation fun! Most dogs just cannot wait for their owners to leave, so they may act like dogs in relative peace.

Moreover, since the dog would have to be stupid to misbehave when the owner is around, it is unlikely the owner will ever again catch the dog in the act of misbehaving. Now, the effectiveness of the owner's next-to-useless, punishment-oriented 'training' program is unquestionably reduced to zero. However, humans are not to be outdone. Just because the dog cannot be punished while misbehaving when the owner is absent, does not mean to say that the dog will not be punished at all. Humans, in all their anthropathetic stupidity, now punish the dog on returning home. Unbelievable! Now we have a dog that spends its day in uncertain expectancy of violent psychological

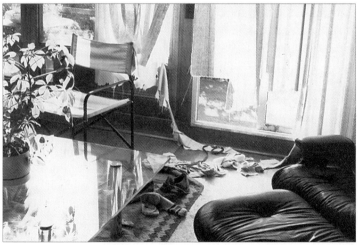

*The remains of Jim's house*

abuse if it greets its owners at the front door. On the one hand, the dog is dying to see its owners, but on the other hand the dog is dreading the owners' return. Pavlov had a wonderful term for this - mental collision! Perhaps the dog muses, "I can't understand it. My owner is fine most of the time, but sometimes without warning and without reason, he attacks. Perhaps it's idiopathic aggression?"

The poor dog is severely stressed, and of course, the cardinal signs of stress are: increased urination frequency, diarrhea and increased general and habitual activity, i.e., the owner's misguided 'treatment' exacerbates the problems. Indeed, the treatment becomes the cause for dogs to run around and frantically chew, dig, bark and soil the house. And Heaven forbid the dog should hide or cringe, when the owner returns home. Obsequious behavior is usually interpreted as signs of guilt, spite and premeditation, all of which prompt more severe punishment.

The Sisyphean task of inhibiting dogs from acting like dogs causes training to degenerate into an endless string of reprimands. The owner's major concern becomes a never-ending quest for different ways to punish the dog. The owner is always asking, "How can I punish the dog for doing this?" or "How can I punish the dog for doing that?" This hardly augurs well for good dog-human relationships, and it is an extremely inefficient way to train a dog.

Remember, for all the ways in which a dog may misbehave and 'get it wrong', there is only one way to get it right! For example, think how many places it is inappropriate for a dog to eliminate. Either we may try to punish the dog for each and every wrong choice - an infinite task which would require an eternity. Or we may teach the dog our choice - the right choice from the outset. The latter takes much less time.

Most dogs have had it up to the gills with reprimands, punishments, negative reinforcement, avoidance training, aversive conditioning and aggravation of that ilk. Have owners ever considered that their poor learner may have a poor teacher? Have owners ever considered that there may be limited knowledge at both ends of the leash? How about a bit of common-sense, show-and-tell, lure/reward training? Why not just resolve the behavior problems, then the owner can give the dog a homecoming hug and plentiful pats after a hard day's work? Since it is the owners who often consider normal dog behavior irksome and inappropriate, the onus lies with owners to teach dogs how to appropriately express their basic doggy nature within the domestic setting.

Try to: 1) restrict potential problems so that its effects are immediately less bothersome, 2) redirect your dog's natural activities to alternative and acceptable outlets, and 3) reward your dog for behaving in an appropriate manner. Most importantly, endeavor to strike a workable compromise with your dog and establish a mutually acceptable and enjoyable living situation.

By adopting a reward-oriented training program, it is seldom necessary to punish your dog at all. The central tenet of any efficacious training program (whether behavior, temperament, or obedience training) is to reward your dog for getting things right. Just think how mad you get when your dog makes mistakes, and instead, praise your dog with 10 times that intensity each time it succeeds. During early education, manipulate the dog's living situation, so that it cannot fail but get things right. Using your brain to lure the dog to voluntarily succeed is easier, more efficient, more effective and much more enjoyable than resorting to brawn to force the dog to comply unwillingly. When presented with a choice: Do it your way and get lotsa goodies or do it the dog's way and get nothing, most dogs soon join the team. Housetraining offers one of the best examples to put these principles to practice.

*The secret for*
*successful housetraining*

# HOUSETRAINING

Whether housebreaking a new puppy or resolving an existing problem in an older dog, the routine is the same: 1) prevent your dog from making mistakes, (i.e., eliminating in inappropriate places), 2) show your dog the appropriate place at the appropriate time, 3) reward your dog for using the appropriate toilet area, and above all 4) teach your dog the relevance of appropriate toilet etiquette.

## 1. Prevent Mistakes

The first time your dog soils your house it creates a precedent - a bad precedent. Subsequent mistakes quickly reinforce the existing bad habit, making it even harder to break. The prime directive of housetraining therefore is to prevent your pup from making mistakes. This is particularly important during the first few days the puppydog is at home. Your puppy's initial elimination sites will remain favorite locations for a long time to come.

A not uncommon housesoiling case history comprises dogs which eliminate in the owner's bedroom - daily! Now, I can understand an owner 'slipping up' and allowing the pup to have a messy mishap once in a while, but not every day! Why not just close the bedroom door and then housetrain the dog. Until a dog is housetrained, surely common sense dictates, it should not have the run of the house, let alone the bedroom! As a temporary solution, at times when you cannot keep an eye on your pup, keep it confined to a single room or an outdoor run.

The purpose of long-term confinement is to confine the problem to a selected area. The owner acknowledges that the pup will need to eliminate sometime during the lengthy confinement period, and so the pup is confined to an area where urine and feces will cause the least damage and provoke the least annoyance, e.g., a utility room or kitchen with non-porous floors, which may be covered with newspaper. The pup soon develops a preference for eliminating on papers in the confinement area. Of course, eventually it will be necessary to break the dog of this habit and train it to eliminate outside exclusively. However, for the meantime, if ever the pup has the run of the house, but the silly owner is not paying attention (i.e., a physically-present but mentally-absent owner), at least the pup is likely to seek out its familiar confinement area when it needs to eliminate, thus causing the least possible damage and inconvenience indoors.

## 2. Teach Appropriate Behavior

Housetraining offers one of the best possible illustrations of the effects of good and bad training techniques. By ignoring the dog's appropriate responses and punishing it for every mistake, housetraining can take forever. There are literally hundreds of different places a puppy can choose to eliminate - all of them hopelessly inappropriate - and the owner must punish the pup for each and every wrong choice. This is unfair and inhumane, especially since punishment for housesoiling tends to be extremely severe. On the other hand, there is only 'one right spot'. So, don't keep it a secret - show it to your dog right away!

## 3. Reward The Dog

Over 95% of housetraining comprises rewarding the dog for eliminating in the right place. If you regularly take your dog to its doggy toilet area and praise it upon completion, the problem will be resolved in short order.

This all sounds fine and dandy in theory, but in practice there's one wee flaw. How do you know in advance when your dog wants to eliminate, so you may escort it to the appropriate area? Here again, confinement comes to the rescue. This time it's short-term close confinement. The most popularly used variations are crate training, tie-downs (short tethers) and place training (confining a dog to its bed, basket, or moveable mat). A crate is the doggy equivalent of a baby's crib or play pen. A tie-down is similar to the principle of a child's car seat, and place training is the equivalent of a well-trained child who can sit still and be quiet on request.

Short-term close confinement temporarily inhibits the pup from eliminating during the short confinement period, such that it is highly likely the pup will need to eliminate immediately upon release. Thus, the purpose of crate-training is to predict the time of elimination, whereupon the pup may be taken directly to its toilet area and be praised for producing.

## Crate Training

Firstly, accustom your puppy to its crate (or tie-down). Leave the crate door open so the pup may come and go as it pleases. Periodically, put treats inside the crate, (dry kibble from tonight's dinner is ideal) so your pup learns the crate is a great place to visit. In fact, have the dog dine in the crate. Praise your dog whenever it visits the crate, and ignore it when it leaves. Then, try closing the door for short periods. Praise your dog, and offer the occasional treat whenever it spends time in its newfound doggy den. Open the door and continue praising your dog, but stop praising and ignore your dog the instant it leaves. The crate will soon become your dog's preferred resting place, whereupon it may be used for confinement.

When away from home, leave your dog in its long-term confinement area and when at home, keep the dog in the crate. Dog crates are easily portable, and so your pup may be confined in the same room as you. Thus, your puppy will not feel excluded or isolated, and you may conveniently keep an eye on the pup to praise it for settling down peacefully or for chewing its chewtoys. Every hour, say "Outside," open the crate door and run your dog to the intended toilet area and then stand still and wait for three minutes. It is likely your dog will eliminate, since it has not done so in the past hour, and the speedy passage to the doggy toilet has jiggled the dog's full bladder and rectum. If your dog pees or poops, praise the living Dickens out of that critter. Drop to your knees (careful where) and THANK THAT DOG! - for its MOST WONDERFUL AND GLORIOUS PERFORMANCE!

Since it is delightfully empty, your puppy may now be allowed the run of the house (under supervision of course) for half an hour or so, before being put back in its crate once more. If your dog does not eliminate within the allotted time-span, no big deal; simply straight back in the crate for another hour and so forth.

Crate-training techniques are so successful that you should consider soliciting the help of a puppy-sitter to housetrain your puppydog as an alternative to long-term confinement when you are away. There must be some nice bloke in the neighborhood who would relish watching over the little tyke. Perhaps an elderly person, who would love to have a dog of his own but does not for some reason. It is important to establish the status quo during the first few weeks your pup is at home. Dog sitters are similarly invaluable when retraining an older dog - just one week of continual crate-training, and the 'problem' never becomes a problem.

If for some reason you do not want to use a crate in training, the same housetraining principles may be applied using tie-downs or place training. A tie-down is a short tether with a clasp at each end. One clasp attaches to the dog's collar and the other to an eye-hook screwed into the baseboard, door jam or floorboards. With a permanent eye-hook in each room, you may move your dog and its mat as you change rooms and so keep an eye on your dog at all times. Some owners find it easier to keep the puppy on leash indoors and tie the leash to their belt. Of course, a diligent owner only needs to instruct the pup to settle down on its mat, which is placed in convenient, easily monitored locations, such as in front of the TV, next to the computer or under the dining room table.

# 4. REALLY REWARD THAT DOG!

Once your dog has been taught the house rules, it needs to learn their relevance. Each time your dog eliminates in the appropriate spot, offering a special training treat is just the ticket. Once your dog realizes its elimination products are the equivalent of coins for a food vending machine, i.e., tokens which may be cashed-in for treats from you simply by eliminating in a designated area, your dog will not want to eliminate anywhere else. Eliminating around the house does not have comparable fringe benefits.

Training treats are especially useful during housetraining because when standing outside in the freezing rain at 6:00 a.m., some owners cannot summon sufficient enthusiasm to smile, let alone to adequately praise a puppy for pooping. However, giving a food treat has the required positive effect. So always keep a screw-top jar of treats handy to your dog's toilet area.

By employing a reward gradient, your dog may even be trained to eliminate in a specific location, i.e., a doggy toilet. The level of the reward varies according to how close your dog eliminates to ground zero: praise for each time your pup eliminates outside; purposeful praise plus a piece of kibble for each time it eliminates within 20 feet of the chosen target; an enthusiastic "Good dog," a meaningful pat and two pieces of kibble for doing it within 10 feet of the target area; a delighted "Gooood dog!," several pets and pats and a training treat  for eliminating within five feet; and for scoring a bull's-eye - five treats, a resounding Woodhousian "WHATTT a good doggie!," multiple hugs and squeezes, promise of a barbecued sheep for supper, extra TV privileges and a free trip to the Bahamas! Eschew litotes; one can never afford to be a master of understatement when housetraining a critter.

Regardless of whether your dog has been trained to eliminate in a specific spot in the backyard or at curbside, a walk still remains one of the best rewards for a defecating dog. People with fenced yards seldom use this valuable reward at all, and people who have no private yard and therefore customarily take the dog outside to eliminate on public property do it all wrong. The common practice of walking a dog to induce it to eliminate is quite awry - the dog gets the walk for free and often, the walk is terminated as soon as the dog relieves itself, i.e., the dog receives one of the biggest rewards in the Western World (a walk) for doing no more than acting like the proverbial banana (in expectation of going walkies), yet it receives the biggest punishment in the civilized canine world (termination of said walk) for doing the right thing in the right place at the right time - going potty on the pavement! We seem to be 180 degrees out of phase here.

Instead, release your dog from its crate, tie-down, or resting place, take it outside and wait

*Eager to get on the go!*

67

for three minutes. If your dog does not eliminate within the allotted time span, back to its doggy den for another hour. However, if your dog does eliminate in its backyard toilet area or in front of the house, it's time for walkies!

Using a walk as a reward is especially important for dogs that eliminate outdoors on public property. Leave the house, stand out front and wait for your dog to eliminate. (Take along a book to read - this book, for example - to pass the time until the dog passes other matters.) If your dog does eliminate in front of the house: 1) it is much easier to clean up after your dog and dispose of the mess in one's own dustbin (i.e., it is no longer necessary to stroll down Main Street handicapped by a bag of doggie doo) and 2) your dog may receive the walk as a reward for eliminating. You will find that a no feces-no walk policy creates a very speedy defecator.

## Mistakes

As far as possible, prevent any mistakes from happening. However, if your pup is ever 'caught in the act', urgently instruct it "Outside!" The single word, "outside," is an instructive reprimand, which immediately conveys two vital bits of information: 1) the tone and volume inform your dog it is about to make a big booboo and 2) the meaning of the word instructs your dog how to make amends. Of course, before using any word as an instructive reprimand, first make certain your dog knows what it means.

Any other reprimand or punishment is much less effective. Saying "No!" is ridiculous when the dog's brain, bladder and bowels all say "Yes." Moreover, a "No" or a guttural "Echh" is non-specific; it merely lets the dog know it is making a mistake but does nothing to inform the dog what is expected. Human temper tantrums, rubbing the dog's nose in the mess or squirting noxious substances in the dog's mouth are all time-consuming, messy and downright cruel. They will only serve to 1) make the dog hand shy and defensive towards the owner and 2) encourage your dog to eliminate in hiding.

"Outside!" is the easiest, quickest, most efficient and most effective way to instructively reprimand your dog.

If you do not catch your dog in the act do NOT reprimand it at all.

The time delay makes it impossible for your dog to comprehend the connection between the crime and punishment. Instead, reprimand yourself - it was your mistake for not having sufficiently confined, supervised or housetrained your dog. Back to step one. Do not pass 'Go,' and do not collect $200. Bad owner! BAD OWNER!!! This will not happen again.

## CHEWING

A single chewing mistake can be extremely expensive. I think the Canine Chewing World Record belongs to a Manhattan Malamute which destroyed over $15,000 worth of furniture and fittings in less than three hours! The cost of chewtoys is minimal compared with the potential cost of misdirected chewing. Consequently, when away from home, leave your pup in its long-term confinement area with a good supply of chewtoys. Not only will this precaution confine any possible chewing activity to that area, but also it will help redirect the puppy's chewing proclivities to appropriate chewtoys, since these are the only chewable objects at hand.

A chewtoy is an item which the dog may chew but cannot destroy or consume. If your dog destroys chewtoys, you will have to pay to

*Phoenix and Oso happily settle down with their stuffed Kongs*

69

replace them. If your dog consumes chewtoys, sooner or later you will be faced with a medical emergency and a large veterinary bill. Use only non-destructible, non-consumable chewtoys. The specific type will depend on your dog.

Which ever type you chose, though, please remember your dog cannot read the label and instructions on the package and so you must actively teach your pup what chewtoys are for. Play chewtoy games: "Take chewtoy," "Fetch chewtoy" and "Find chewtoy." It is a good plan to have a toy box in a permanently accessible location, so your pup knows where it can always find a toy should it be in need of a quick chew. Above all, praise and reward your pup whenever it plays with one of its toys.

Inappropriate chewing is seldom an issue when the owner is home; it is almost exclusively an owner-absent problem (created by the owner), which primarily occurs immediately after the owner has left in the morning and immediately before the owner returns in the afternoon/evening. Dogs are crepuscular and are normally most active at dawn and dusk. Most dogs dare not chew whilst the owner is at home, and so in the mornings it eagerly awaits the owner's departure to indulge its chewing habit. (Much like a person looking forward to the spouse's morning departure in anticipation of the first illegal cigarette of the day.) In the afternoons, the dog chews partly as its activity level increases and partly to quell the stress created by the prospect of punishment upon the owner's return. Ensuring that your pup is engrossed with a chewtoy, both at the time of your departure and prior to your return, goes a long way to preventing owner-absent house destruction.

## When Leaving

Before departing in the morning, give your pup a novel chewtoy. The novelty, and hence the value, of the chewtoy may be enhanced in a number of ways. Rawhide toys may be soaked in different flavored soups. Let them dry and voila! - a different flavored chewtoy for each morning of the week. Alternatively, tasty treats may be squished into the marrow cavity of a large (indestructible), open-ended knuckle bone or Kong chewtoy. Sterilized bones and

Kongs are available from most pet shops. Stuff the chewtoys so some treats fall out fairly easily as your dog chews, but other treats never come out, prompting your dog to continue to work at the chewtoy.

Make sure to leave your pup in its long-term confinement area, littered with stuffed chewtoys. This is like leaving a child and a television in an empty room. The child will watch the box and become a TV addict. Similarly, the pup will chew the chewtoys (since there is precious else to do) and develop a chewtoy habit, because chewing novel and attractive chewtoys quickly becomes self-reinforcing. This process is a form of passive training , whereby all you have to do is set up the situation, and the dog all but trains itself to become a chewtoyaholic

## When Returning

On returning home, the best reward is yourself, and so delay greeting your pup until it fetches a chewtoy. Within a few days, you will be greeted at the front door by your puppy doing an impersonation of a retriever with a dumbbell. Thus, when your pup wakes up and becomes re-energized in the afternoon, it will search for a chewtoy in anticipation of the forthcoming attention and affection upon your return. The ritual is facilitated if you take the proffered chewtoy, extricate the squished treats (with a pencil) and give them to the pup.

When at home, always try to reinforce your puppy's chewtoy habit with further passive training. Confine your pup to its crate, tie-down, or place, with the only object in reach being a chewtoy stuffed with all sorts of goodies. This is so important with young puppies during their first few days at home, since they quickly become fixated on the first few objects they chew and play with.

Once your pup knows what it should be chewing, it is time to let it know what it should not be chewing. Every time the pup even sniffs a likely alternative, the instructive reprimand "Chewtoy!" will quickly set the puppy straight. The tone and volume inform the pup it is about to make a booboo, and the meaning of the word instructs the pup what it should be chewing. In addition, it is a good idea to boobytrap prime chewing targets.

## Boobytraps

A well-designed boobytrap has a number of significant attributes. Firstly, boobytraps are effective at times when owners are absent. Secondly, the dog is punished by the boobytrap and not by its owner. Thus, the dog may be effectively punished without risking the danger of ruining the relationship between owner and dog. Boobytraps are extremely effective because of the immediacy and relevancy of the punishment. A good boobytrap startles the dog the moment it transgresses. The dog is punished by the environment. The dog investigates the environment, and the environment is unfriendly. It is similar to a dog putting its nose into a candle flame - it only does it once. With boobytraps, learning is often a one-trial process.

The types of boobytrap may be many and varied and are limited only by the imagination and ingenuity of the owner/designer. My favorite designs all incorporate numerous empty beer cans. The same basic principle may be applied to protect a variety of objects - armchairs, carpets, children's toys, food on the table, and garbage cans. Twenty or so beer cans (each containing a couple of pebbles for maximum rattle-effect) are stacked on a sheet of cardboard, which is placed on top of three other cans, one of which is balanced on the edge of a shelf or counter, overhanging the object to be protected, e.g., the kitchen garbage. A piece of string links the precariously balanced support-can to the bait, e.g., a piece of paper dipped in chicken broth or bacon fat, which is laid on top of crumpled newspaper which fills the garbage can. When the dog grabs the bait, the string tugs out one of the bottom three beer cans, causing the cardboard to tilt and all the other beer cans to crash around the dog.

Since we do not want to live in a house which is permanently boobytrapped, set up the booby trap but do not connect the trip wire. Give the dog time to get used to the presence of the boobytrap. Otherwise, the dog will make the connection between the booby trap and the falling cans, i.e., it will stay away from the garbage when the cans are present, but trash the garbage when you have dismantled the booby trap.

The effectiveness of any boobytrap is improved with the addition of a warning cue. Immediately prior to arming the booby trap, wipe the garbage container with a novel odor, e.g., a new lemon-scented cleaner or perfume, or any odorous substance the dog has never previously encountered. Since the dog has trashed successfully many times before, but this time the world dropped on its head, it will no doubt surmise "Ahhh! The smell. That's what's different." The dog quickly makes the connection between the novel odor and the falling beer cans. Now, the olfactory warning cue - the new cleaner - may be applied to other objects where the dog's nose is not desired, such as counter tops, chair legs, the cat's litter box and the underside of carpets. The odor warns the dog: touch this and beer cans are likely to drop on your head, so the dog doesn't touch. The effectiveness of avoidance conditioning lies with the warning cue; the warning cue deters the dog from touching the protected item, and so at a later date, it never learns the boobytrap is no longer armed.

## DIGGING

Dogs need to dig. There are a dozen good canine reasons for digging: digging warming pits and cooling hollows, excavating feline feces, grubs, roots and rodents, digging to escape, digging out of boredom, digging for fun, and of course, the quintessential canine bona fide reason - burying bones and then, digging them up again. Also please bear in mind, many dogs dig from boredom of their solitary confinement in the backyard because the owner dare not leave the dog indoors. Often housetraining and chewtoy training offer simple solutions to digging and barking problems.

*Cerberus guarding the entrance to Hades*

When you cannot supervise your puppy, confine it to an area where it cannot dig, for example indoors or to an outdoor run. When you can work with the pup, actively redirect its digging activities to an appropriate area, e.g., a digging pit.

## A Digging Pit

From your viewpoint, the pup is digging in the wrong place and so to be fair, provide a location that you find appropriate and then teach your puppy to use it. A digging pit is much like a child's sand pit. To teach your pup to enjoy digging in its pit, keep it well stocked with all sorts of goodies: stashes of kibble, the odd training treat, chewtoys (yes, we need them outdoors as well), tennis balls, squeaky toys, and maybe even a cow's femur. Once your pup learns its digging pit is a virtual treasure trove, it will much rather dig there than in the rest of the yard. What's so marvelous about unearthing a root or a dead slug, when there are bones and chunks of freeze-dried liver to be found in the pit? I mean, what's the point of prospecting for gold in New Jersey, when it was discovered in California? Digging in the pit quickly becomes self-reinforcing, and finding treasure is especially rewarding. Even so, continue to praise and reward your pup each time it digs in its pit.

Appropriate digging may also be taught via a passive learning process. Confined to a concrete run with a digging pit at one end, a potential digger soon develops the good habit of digging in its pit (because there is nowhere else to dig). After a couple of weeks, the door of the run may be left open and the dog will likely seek out its digging pit whenever it feels an excavatory urge.

If you plan to leave your dog unattended in the yard for long periods of time, then beforehand you must spend some time with the dog outside, teaching it the rules of the yard, for example, to not even walk on the garden, let alone dig in it. Should you see your dog about to dig in the lawn, the instructive reprimand "Digging Pit!" adequately informs the dog that it is doing something wrong and where it should be digging.

# BARKING

No one would think of putting a shock collar on a canary, squirting lemon juice into a baby's mouth or beating a husband with a rolled-up newspaper and having his vocal cords cut for 'singing' in the shower. However, people think nothing of doing all of these and more to barking dogs. Barking poses particular problems because owners are consistently inconsistent. Sometimes the dog is allowed to bark. Sometimes it is encouraged to bark, yet other times it is severely punished for barking. It is all so confusing and stressful for the poor dog. No wonder the dog lets rip when the owner is away from home.

If your dog barks when you are away from home, for goodness sake do not confine it outdoors. In fact, outdoor confinement likely precipitated the problem in the first place. Sound carries. If confined outside, your dog will more easily hear outside disturbances, and your neighbors will be more easily disturbed by the dog's barking. Until the barking problem has been resolved, restrict barking by confining your dog indoors, preferably to a single room (to reduce activity), away from the street (to reduce the effect of outside disturbances) and on the opposite side of the house from complaining

neighbors (to reduce complaints). Draw the curtains in the confinement area and otherwise insulate for sound. Leave a radio playing fairly loudly to reassure the dog and to provide white noise, which will help muffle sounds from outdoors and disguise the dog's barking.

*Malamutes howl - What else is new?*

75

When at home, it is easier and less confusing to start with a single rule: barking is OK until the dog is instructed to "Shush," whereupon it is expected to be quiet for a specified time - say one or two minutes - after which, most dogs will have forgotten what sparked them off in the first place. The first

step in training your dog to decrease the frequency of barking is to teach it to bark on command. This may sound a little silly; however, it is important to realize that barking is a temporal problem, i.e., the dog barks excessively, or it barks at inappropriate times. By training your dog to bark on command,

*Callahan learns to Speak and Shush!*     at least you establish

partial temporal control over the behavior. Also, once barking is under stimulus control, it becomes possible to instruct your dog to bark at times when it may not feel like barking, which greatly facilitates teaching the more important "Shush" command.

## Bark on Command

Select a stimulus which prompts your dog to bark, e.g., the doorbell. Station an accomplice outside the front door. Instruct your dog to "Alert" or "Defend" (more impressive commands than "Sing" or "Speak"), which is the cue for your accomplice to ring the door bell, which in turn prompts your dog to bark. Your dog will quickly learn to anticipate the sound of the doorbell following your command and after just half a dozen or so repetitions, the command "Defend" will be sufficient to prompt your dog to bark. This is the type of training exercise that may give a guard dog an insecurity complex. "How on earth does the owner always know when the doorbell is about to ring? I'm going to lose my job unless I bark when the owner says Defend."

## Shush!

At a time when your dog has no cause to give voice, instruct it to bark and profusely praise it for doing so. This practice alone pleasantly surprises most dogs, especially if you join in and sing along. Then, instruct your dog to "Shush," and waggle a food treat in front of its nose. Once your dog stops barking to sniff (it is impossible to sniff and bark simultaneously), offer the treat and gently praise your dog for eating quietly. Talking in whispers will encourage your dog to listen, and if it listens, it will be unlikely to bark, otherwise it would not be able to hear what it is listening to. Using the treat as a lure/hand signal to entice your dog to sit and/or lie down will also help the dog settle down and shush. After only a couple of seconds of silence, tell the dog to bark again - a second pleasant surprise for the dog. No matter how difficult it was getting the dog to shut up the first time, it will be much easier the second time. Then, tell it to bark again - "Good dog Rover, good woofs" and then instruct it to "Shush" - "Good dog Rover, goooood shhhhushhhh." Repeatedly turn the dog 'on' and 'off,' and praise and reward the dog both for barking and for being quiet. Fait accompli!

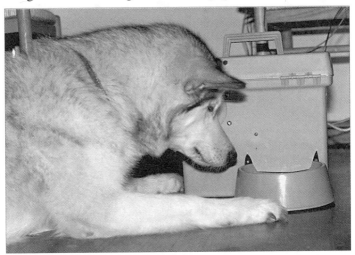

*Phoenix autoshapes herself to settle down and shush*
*from the Watson/Dunbar Computerized Bark Box*

77

Now, your trained dog may be allowed to be a dog and bark until instructed to "Shush." You may now begin to modify your dog's barking sprees by teaching specific rules about barking: 1) in response to which stimuli the dog must bark, e.g., strangers, doorbell, etc., 2) to which stimuli it is allowed to bark (a little), e.g., a cat in the yard (come on, let's be fair!), 3) for how long it is allowed to bark in each instance (e.g., at least 10 woofs for someone at the front door, but only a maximum of three to four woofs for a neighborhood cat or dog), and 4) to which stimuli the dog is not allowed to give voice, e.g., an oak leaf falling three blocks away - hardly a world-shattering event that needs to be heralded by several hundred woofs!

## JUMPING-UP

Jumping-up is primarily a problem of adolescent and adult dogs. Puppies jump-up, but owners rarely see it as a problem. In fact, many owners unintentionally encourage puppy jumping.

For dogs that jump-up to greet people, a variety of dog training texts recommend the owner: shout at the dog, squirt it in the face with water or lemon juice, swat it on the nose with a rolled-up newspaper, yank on the dog's leash, hang the dog by its choke-collar, squeeze the dog's front paws, tread on its hind paws, knee it in the chest or flip it over backwards. Surely, this is all a little excessive for a dog that's only trying to say hello. Confucius once said, "There is no need to use an axe to remove a fly from the forehead of a friend." Why not just train your dog to sit or lie down when greeting people?

## Etiology

Dogs jump-up for a variety of reasons. First and foremost, most dogs have been trained to jump-up since puppyhood. When the young pup jumped and pawed, most people patted it on the head and scratched it behind the ear, because they were too lazy to bend down to puppy level. And then one day the dog dutifully jumps-up to greet its owner, who in turn greets the friendly furry with a whop on the bonce or a knee in the chest. The dog's only crime? It grew!

Pawing, licking and jumping-up are all friendly appeasement gestures - the dog's way of saying "Welcome home. Pleased to see

78

you. Please accept my presence. Please don't hurt me - I'm a lowly worm compared with you most honored human!" And so what does the most honored human do? But punish the dog for jumping up! Now, of course, the dog has two reasons to show deference - the initial reason and the fact it must now appease its angry owner. And how does it try to appease the owner? By pawing, licking and jumping-up! This is one of the many paradoxes in training - the more one punishes the dog, the more the behavior increases in frequency. Again, the 'treatment' is the cause.

## Counterconditioning

Right from the outset, reward-train your puppy to sit-stay when greeting people. Rather than trying to extinguish complicated social behaviors with punishment, it is easier to employ a simple counterconditioning procedure and train your pup to perform an alternative and acceptable greeting behavior - one which is mutually exclusive to the problem behavior, i.e., the puppy cannot sit and jump-up at the same time. If your pup sits and stays, you may praise it both for sitting and for not jumping-up. If your pup jumps-up however, you have yet to train it to sit-stay properly and so, back to step one.

Counterconditioning procedures sound like the symphony of simplicity. And they are - in theory. However, it can be a little more challenging to put theory to practice. For many dogs, the word 'uncontrollable' is a kindly euphemism for their behavior when greeting people. Many dogs are so excited and distracted that they fail to acknowledge their owner's very existence, let alone respond obediently to any request to "Sit." Counterconditioning is the theoretical answer, but troubleshooting is the practical solution.

## Troubleshooting

With extreme behavior problems, it is next to impossible to train a dog during the course of everyday living. For example, it is difficult to train a puppy to sit, when returning home from a heavy, harried, hassled and otherwise quite horrible day at work. Similarly, it is a poor percentage procedure to try and train the dog to sit at the front door when a visitor arrives. When the owner is in a hurry to open the door and pays only marginal attention to the dog, the dog in turn pays less-than-marginal attention to its owner. However, by troubleshooting the problem, you may set aside a convenient and specific time to teach your puppy how it is expected to act when greeting people.

Teach your pup to sit, using a lure/reward training method and proof the pup's response, especially in the front hallway and on-leash outdoors, i.e., in places where your dog normally greets people. Indoors, the dog may be additionally trained to sit in a specific place, e.g., on a mat in the front hall. With one owner watching the dog in a sit-stay on its mat, another owner may periodically open and close the front door and repeatedly ring the doorbell to get the dog used to distractions specifically associated with a visitor's arrival. If we are going to expect the dog to sit when greeting people, we must make sure that the dog at least knows how to "Sit-stay" in similar but less distracting circumstances.

## Greeting You

Firstly - the difficult part - on returning home, instruct your dog to sit (or lie down) on its mat, and delay greeting the dog until it does so. If good Rover sits, gently praise the dog to excess. If bad Rover does not sit, keep trying until he does so. Do what it takes - take hold of the dog's collar and keep hold until the dog complies. This is no more difficult than routinely dealing with the dog in everyday distracting situations. Only this time, you shall persevere, and eventually, your dog will sit and be suitably praised for its trouble. Other reprimands and punishments are neither necessary nor advisable. Your dog will soon learn he has to sit before you will deign to say hello. Indeed, as soon as your dog sits, greet it with gentle stroking, calm but profuse praise and a couple of food treats.

Now comes the easy part. Once your dog's exuberance has waned following the customary exultation of sniffs, licks, wags and wiggles, slip out of the house by the back door, 'return home' via the front door once more and request Rover to go to the appropriate place and assume the appropriate position, i.e., to sit on his mat. This time, however, it will be much, much easier to get Rover to sit. Rover is not nearly as excited by your return, because he has only just greeted you seconds beforehand. After greeting your dog for the second time, leave and repeat the procedure a third time, and then once more and so on. Rover's performance will improve with each repeated re-entry.

With repeated exposures to the same stimulus complex (owner at front door), your dog will become less and less excited and therefore he will become progressively easier to control. It will become easier and easier to get your dog to sit with subsequent repetitions. Using troubleshooting procedures, the initial improvement is dramatic. Once Rover's performance is impeccable, repeat the departure/arrival sequence another half a dozen or so times in order to leave an utterly indelible impression on your dog's brain - that you are thoroughly pleased and overjoyed with your dog's newly learned (newly taught) social etiquette and mannerly greetings.

Troubleshooting is especially important for dogs which are kept outside for any reason. An outdoors dog will generally go bonkers when it comes inside. This, of course, is often a primary reason why the dog was relegated outdoors in the first place. A vicious circle quickly develops. The more the dog is kept outside, the greater its exuberance and the worse its behavior whenever it comes indoors. Eventually, the dog will be kept outdoors permanently. Whether you want the dog to be able to come indoors in a mannerly fashion or whether you want to be able to venture into your own backyard without being blitzed by Bozo, the troubleshooting procedures are similar.

Invite your dog indoors and instruct him to "Settle Down and Shush." Once the dog has calmed down, instruct him to go "Outside" again. Have the dog come inside and go outside several times in a row. Not only does this procedure improve the dog's demeanor and deportment on each successive ingress, but also it increases the dog's eagerness for each successive egress. The dog learns to come inside like a civilized canine, and it learns that having to go outside does not necessarily mean it will be left out in the cold 'till the ends of time. When your dog eventually enters in an impeccable, orderly fashion, let it stay awhile.

For dogs living permanently outdoors, go out to greet the dog several times in a row. The first visit will be a disaster. The second will be merely unpleasant. The third will be pretty good, and on the fourth and subsequent visits, the dog will be well behaved. So if the dog's so perfect, why not bring him indoors for company, comfort and protection? Yea owner!

## Greeting the Owner with Feeling

Some owners feel there are times when it is both appropriate and enjoyable for their dog to greet them by jumping-up. To avoid confusion, always herald these occasions with a suitable request, e.g., "Give us a Hug." Never allow the dog to jump-up unless on invitation. When returning home, first have the dog greet you in a calm, controlled stay, and then once you have closed the front door or changed into dog-jumping clothes, tell the dog to give you a hug. Thus, the previous problem - joyful jumping - becomes the reward for not jumping-up during the initial greeting.

*Give us a hug!*

*Mmmmm!*

# Greeting Visitors

Invite 20 friends over, ostensibly to watch a football game on the television but in reality, for a Rover-training extravaganza. When Patrick arrives, it is possible to direct 110% of your attention towards your dog, because there is no hurry to open the door - it's a set-up, and anyway, it's only Patrick! It doesn't matter how long it takes to get your dog to sit or lie-down. Take encouragement. The first time will be the hardest, and from then on, it will be as easy as teaching a possum to play dead. Once the dog is sitting (or lying) on its mat, instruct Patrick to enter. (The door is closed but unlocked, and so there is no need to divert attention from your dog.) Continually praise your dog all the time it remains sitting on its mat. Pat may offer a hand for your dog to sniff and a food treat for your dog to eat. Tell Pat to go and sit down in the living room, and then, instruct Rover to say hello. Pat may pat the pooch and allow it to perform the requisite nose-scan of all the olfactory goodies that normally reside on visitors' clothing (the intoxicating smell of Pat's cute Pyrenees) and on the undersoles of their shoes (the remains of that otherwise mighty mound of Corgi copros, which Pat squished on the corner of Folker and 46th).

Once Rover has settled down and got used to Pat's presence, Pat should make a surreptitious exit and then ring the doorbell once more. Characteristically, the dog will make a wild and woolly rush to the door with all the uncontrolled exuberance of before, only to calm down a mite when it realizes it is only Pat again. Since the dog is calmer, it is more easily and quickly controlled. Pat enters, gives the dog a treat and then sits down to allow the dog a cursory olfactory investigation. This time your dog will not be quite as intent on nose-vacuuming Pat's pants and soles but will settle down more quickly. Exit Pat stage right, only to ring the doorbell again. A rapid rush by Rover, but then those familiar footsteps, the rhythm of the ring, the cadence of the clapper, a quick sniff at the bottom of the door, a glimpse of Pat's ugly mug and the sober realization - "Pat! Are you coming or going?" Since Patrick's presence is now no more distracting than a spare pair of mukluks, it is easy to control Rover and to get him to sit-stay on the mat. Rover gets it right, and so,

Rover gets rewarded. Therefore Rover will be more likely to get it right in the future. Pat should leave and return a few more times for good luck, then settle down to warm up the TV and drink down some cold beers (to empty cans for booby traps). Have Pat perform a total of 10 re-entries during the course of the football game. (Keep the beers on the porch as an incentive for visitors to make repeated trips outdoors.)

Now it is time to call Susan and repeat the entire multiple-entry program. And then with Tammy, and then Stacie, *et alia,* until the whole crew is assembled to watch the game on the box. Within just a single session of concentrated greeting (some 200 greetings with 20 people in under four hours), Rover will learn how to greet visitors at the front door, and you will learn how to control your dog, such that things will be much easier on Monday morning with real visitors from back East. (Or from out West. It works just as well with visitors from all points of departure.) It may be necessary to occasionally touch-up training in the future. If your dog molests any visitors, just ask them to leave and come back in again.

## Strangers on the Street

A similar troubleshooting ploy may be designed to teach your dog how to appropriately greet strangers on the street. Again, it is difficult to train your dog effectively during the course of everyday living, e.g., when rushing to post a letter. Instead, at half-time in the ballgame, supply each of your 20 visitors with treats for the dog and then turf them out on the streets with instructions to space out and walk clockwise around the block. You and your dog can set off in a counter-clockwise direction. When meeting each person, request your dog to sit. If the dog sits, praise the good critter, and maybe offer a treat. Also, the ersatz strangers may praise your dog and gently pet it. If your dog jumps-up, instructively reprimand him - "SIT!" Your dog has a choice: 1) sit and receive praise, pats and treats or 2) jump-up and be reprimanded, yet have to sit anyway, i.e., Hobson's choice. Your dog will happily elect to sit.

The first lap around the block often resembles a post-touchdown pantomime with the dog trying to high-five (or high-four-forepaw)

*Oso and Phoenix sit to greet guests*

each person it encounters. However, by only the second or third lap, your dog begins to get the idea how to greet people. By the fourth or fifth lap, the dog is perfect.

Try this exercise with a couple of groups of people. In this fashion, it is possible to practice a hundred or so street encounters within the half-hour. Your dog has been given the opportunity to master the required domestic social graces when meeting strangers, so that when on the way to post a letter, you will have better control when meeting real strangers.

# III. OBEDIENCE TRAINING

## *Requiem for Rover. Act III. Scene i*

*Rover was a wonderful puppy. As soon as he had completed his series of puppy shots, the owners took him to the park and let him off-leash to run. Rover ran and romped and pranced and pounced like a wound-up whirling dervish. When Rover was spent, exhausted and happy, he returned to his equally happy owners, who put him on leash and took him home. As a puppy, Rover had a ball.*

*As Rover approached adolescence, half-an-hour of romping in the park barely dented his enthusiasm, and he was not ready to stop playing when his owners wanted to go home. So the owners called Rover. In good faith, Rover went to his owners to check out what they wanted. And... "Son of a female dog!", if they didn't put him on leash and take him home! "But I hadn't finished playing..."*

*Now, Rover was hardly a great philosopher, but on the other hand, he wasn't as stooopid as his owners. He quickly arrived at an effective solution. "I've really got to pay attention to these owners when I'm playing, and as soon as they say the dreaded words, "Come Here," I must keep away at all cost." The owners tried to catch Rover, but his speed had improved along with his endurance. Rover had a riot. Rover thought 'Tag' was a wonderful game. The owners didn't. And when they eventually grabbed Rover, they were not exactly in the best of spirits; the owners shook poor Rover and shouted most terrible things. Oh Dear! I bet Rover will be really keen to let his owners grab him next time he's running in the park. Sadly though, the days of park-outings were numbered.*

# Scene ii

Even though Rover was utterly out of control, his owners still let him off-leash to play. They made excuses for the dog's disobedience. "Well, he comes sometimes. But he always does it at home. He's very strong-willed you know." The very next outing, Rover chased a cat across the street. The cat made it; Rover didn't. Rover was hit by a car.

# Scene ii (Alternate A)

Rover chased a cat across the street in front of an oncoming car. Both Rover and the cat made it. The car didn't. The car driver swerved to miss Rover and hit a tree. The car was a write-off. So were the passengers. (The largest judgment ever levied against a dog owner is $2,700,000. The dog ran into the street, causing a pick-up truck to swerve. The two passengers were thrown from the truck and suffered severe head injuries and brain damage.)

# Scene ii (Alternate B)

Nobody in the family could control Rover when he was off-leash, and so wisely, family members decided to walk him on-leash. Now, Rover dearly missed his off-leash turbo-romps, and so he 'walked' on-leash in much the same fashion. Sprained digits, tendonitis in the elbow and partially subluxated shoulder joints progressively took their toll on the family members until there were no volunteers to walk Rover at all. Anyway, the novelty had worn off. Rover was no longer a cute, cuddly, controllable puppy. Rover played hardball now.

Because Rover missed his daily owner-drag around the block, the activity level of indoor romps increased to dangerous and unbearable proportions. Consequently, Rover was now confined to the yard for much of the time and was only let inside on special occasions. Whenever friends and relatives came to visit, the owners would call Rover and put *him outside. The canine cerebrum calculates, "Whenever they say those words 'Come Here', they throw me outside, and I miss all the fun." Rover was impossible to catch. On the few occasions he was allowed indoors, he was utterly beside himself with joy and ran to greet his long-lost family members with enthusiasm. He ran round and round the house (just like he had been encouraged to do in the park as a puppy) knocking over chairs, knocking over children and grandparents, jumping on visitors, and torpedo-goosing, pawing and licking them to death. Rover was relegated to the yard for good. The good old suburban backyard - the canine theatre for a best and last performance of Act II.*

*The owners set the precedent for hyperactive rambunctiousness right from the getgo. Again, Rover's only crime was that he grew. He got bigger and stronger, and his activity level and endurance became intolerable for the family. His over-rambunctiousness made him a difficult prospect to train. Moreover, because the owners made a distinction between fun and training and because Rover thought fun and training were mutually exclusive, Rover voted for fun. For Rover, having a good time - running and playing with other dogs - became a preferred alternative and a severe distraction to training. Unfortunately, Rover's fun was to become a fleeting puppyhood memory. Rover had a good time... for a short time. And now, Rover has an extremely short life-expectancy.*

Establish an acceptable status quo from the beginning. A young pup is extremely impressionable and can easily learn, for example, that there are times for little quiet moments. Once you can get your adolescent dog to settle down with a single request and once you can control your dog's behavior, no matter what it is doing or how worked up it may be, there is a lifetime of fun ahead. Well-trained Rover can accompany you on walks, runs, picnics, drives, visiting relatives, staying at motels, summer cabins etc. A little forethought and control with your puppy, and Rover can then enjoy life - for the rest of his long life.

In order to produce a reliably trained dog with the minimum of owner-effort, you must teach your dog the relevance of obedience instructions, in addition to their meaning. Once your dog understands the relevance of complying to your requests, reprimands will be seldom necessary. Integrate training with your dog's especially enjoyable activities right from the outset. Thus, rather than becoming distractions which work against training, playing with other dogs and all other enjoyable doggy-activities become rewards which work for training.

## SIT, DOWN AND STAND

### 1. Sit

Weigh out your puppydog's daily diet and take a handful of kibble. Give one piece to the pup to let it know 'the game's afoot', say "Rover, Sit" and then slowly move a second training treat upwards and backwards over the pup's head, keeping it close to its nose. As your pup lifts its head to follow the food, it will sit down. When the dog sits down, give it the food lure as a reward. Magic? No, just

*Dimity the PBGV learns to sit during the filming of an episode of It's a Dog's Life.*

*Using the 'stairs method'*
*to lure the dogs down from the sit.*

quadrupedial vertebrate structural engineering. Basically, it is impossible for most quadrupeds to look directly upwards without sitting down. We call this 'the coyote howling at the moon' posture. Try this on yourself. Stand like a dog (or a football lineman) with arms and legs straight and toes and fingers on the ground and then try to look up at a point on the ceiling directly overhead. This is impossible without: either raising one's fingers off the ground, or by bending the legs and sitting down.

If your pup raises its forepaws off the ground during this exercise, you are holding the food treat too high. Lower the treat and move it backwards between its eyes only an inch above its head. (To teach the pup to sit on its haunches or stand on its hind legs please see the section on Tricks.) If your dog backs up, perform the exercise in a corner.

## 2. Down

With your puppydog sitting, say "Rover Down." Let it sniff another food treat, and then quickly lower the lure to the ground between the pup's forepaws. Most dogs assume a 'playbow' posture - forequarters lowered with sternum on the ground and hindquarters stuck up in the air as if they are mooning the moon. (You may teach your pup to 'bow' at a later date. See Tricks.) By slowly moving the treat: either a few inches forwards away from the pup's forepaws, or backwards between its forelegs towards the dog's chest, the rump will lower to the ground, and your pup will lie down. When the puppy lies down, give it the treat as a reward.

If your puppy stands up instead, just start over from the beginning. At this stage of training, reprimands would be utterly inappropriate, since the puppy has no idea what we are trying to teach, and so as yet, it is not doing anything wrong. Neither is it doing it right. So, back to square one and start over.

## 3. Sit Again

With the puppy lying down, say "Rover Sit," let it sniff another training treat and then move the lure upwards and backwards over the pup's head. Your pup will push itself up into the sitting position. You may have to waggle the treat or clap your hands over the pup's head to energize it to sit up. Enticing the larger 'sack 'o potato' breeds to sit up can take no small amount of enthusiasm and mental energy on the part of the trainer. So, get enthusiastic! Once your pup sits, give it the treat for its effort.

## 4. Stand

Let your sitting pup sniff another lure, say "Rover Stand" and then move the treat forwards and away from the pup, keeping the treat at nose level and moving it parallel to the ground. Your pup will stand. As soon as it does so, lower the treat a mite to get the pup to look down, otherwise it might sit again. However, do not lower the treat too far, otherwise your puppy will lie down. Give your pup the treat once it stands steadily.

## 5. Lie Down Again

With your pup standing, say "Rover Down." Lower a treat to the ground to a spot between the pup's forepaws, and once your pup lowers its head, slowly move the lure backwards between its forelegs, and the rump will collapse. If the pup backs up, perform the exercise in a corner. This is

*Using a chewtoy under the leg to lure Oso down from the stand*

the hardest of all the body-position changes, and so be patient and persevere. Remember, the first time is always the hardest. Once the pup has done it just a couple of times, it will be as easy as falling off a log.

# 6. Stand Again

Say "Rover Stand," take another treat and move it diagonally upwards and forwards away from the pup's nose, and the dog will stand. You may have to waggle the treat to energize the pup and entice it to stand. Once your pup stands, lure it to look down a tad so that it does not sit, and then give it the treat once it stands steadily.

## Sit/Down/Stand Sequences

Vary the order of the body position commands at random, or by using the following, easy-to-remember test sequences:

1. sit-down-sit-stand-down-stand
2. sit-stand-sit-down-stand-down
3. down-sit-down-stand-sit-stand

Varying at least three different body positions increases the speed with which the pup learns verbal commands. If we alternated just two body positions, e.g., sit and down - 'doggy push-ups', the pup would quickly become bored with endless repetition, and it would anticipate each command rather than listen to the owner's instructions. For example, the pup quickly learns, if it is sitting, the next command must be "Down." Varying the order of instructions increases your puppy's attentiveness and concentration.

For the first sequence only, reward your pup following each change of body position. On the second sequence, reward after every other change, then after three changes and so on until the pup performs an entire sequence of six responses for just one reward. After only a few trials, a single food reward is more than sufficient for your pup to perform several complete sequences in succession. Do no more than five repetitions at any one time, and reserve food rewards for those special responses performed with particular pizzazz and panache.

Repeat the above sequences at least 50 times a day, until you and the pup are picture-perfect. Do NOT do all repetitions at once, or else you will bore your dog silly. Also, performing the exercises in a single training session produces a dog which is only reliable at training times, for example in the kitchen before dinner. To create a dog which is reliable at all times, you must train it at all times in a wide variety of settings. To accomplish this with minimal expenditure of effort and energy, integrate training into your daily routine. Call your dog and perform just one sequence: each time you turn on the stove, open the fridge, make a cup of tea or go to the bathroom, when the clock chimes, when you turn a page of a magazine, book or newspaper, when you turn on the television and during each commercial break and whenever you think of it. Similarly, when walking the dog, perform a single sequence: before putting on and taking off the dog's leash, each time you go through a door or gate, each time you see another dog or person, each time you pass a lamppost or fire hydrant, before and after crossing the street and, whenever you think of it. You will find it easy to have several hundred mini-training sessions each day without deviating too much from your daily routine. Moreover, when your puppy collides with adolescence, you will find your daily routine runs smoother with a well-trained dog.

## PHASING OUT LURES AND REWARDS

Whether you know it or not, what you have been doing here is using food treats in two extremely useful ways: as lures to entice your pup into different body positions and as rewards for the pup to reinforce correct responses when it promptly moves into the desired position. Certainly, food is one of the very best possible lures to entice a dog to perform a variety of responses without coercion, and food is a pretty effective reward for most dogs. A lure/reward training method, especially one employing training treats both as lures and rewards, is without out a doubt the quickest, easiest, most efficient, most effective and most enjoyable way to complete the first two stages of training: 1) to teach the dog the meaning of our instructions and 2) to teach the dog the relevance of our instructions.

Whereas one can never give too many food treats during temperament training exercises, many owners are seduced by the effectiveness of food training when teaching obedience and 1) fail to wean themselves from using food as a lure and 2) give far too many food treats as rewards. Owners quickly become dependent on using food as a lure, since they feel the dog will not comply otherwise. And sure enough, the dog's compliance quickly becomes contingent on the owner having food in the hand. Similarly, giving too many rewards in training is the quickest way to decrease their value and produce a 'spoiled dog'.

Food lures and rewards are so valuable in training that it would be unfair to the dog and masochistic for the owner not to use food. However, the number one item on the training agenda is to begin to phase out food as soon as the pup responds correctly, i.e., following the pup's very first sit! Obviously, no one wants to carry around a smorgasbord of doggie treats for the rest of the pup's life in order to get it to respond obediently. Food may always remain an occasional ingredient of any training program - as a special reward for the occasional excellent response and always as a lure for teaching any new exercise. However, it is important the dog's willingness to perform is not contingent on the owner having food or other lures and rewards.

The dog must be convinced that it wants to comply by teaching it the relevance of our requests. Otherwise, the puppy's initial dramatic learning spree will be followed by an equally dramatic forgetting junket. Just because the pup knows the meaning of our requests does not mean it will necessarily respond. Although food is usually a pretty good reward for most dogs during initial training in non-distracting circumstances, it may not be as effective, if for example the pup would rather play with other dogs. By integrating training into the life of the dog, food rewards may be progressively phased out and substituted with much more valuable and relevant life rewards. Thus, the puppy learns the relevance of our requests and wants to comply.

Substituting food lures with verbal commands and hand signals comprises the first stage of training - teaching the meaning of instructions. Once the pup has learned the meaning of verbal commands and handsignals, it is no longer necessary to use food as a lure to get it to respond, since the word 'sit' has become a verbal lure and the lure/hand movement has become a hand signal. Substituting food rewards with more valuable life-rewards comprises the second stage of training - teaching the relevance of following our instructions.

From the outset, alternate sessions using food as a lure only with sessions using food as a reward only. Your dog will quickly learn: 1) just because you have a goodie in your hand does not necessarily mean it will get it and 2) sometimes it will receive a treat when it responds correctly, even if you did not have one in your hand.

## Phasing Out Food Lures

With food treats in a shirt pocket and without food in the hand, ask your pup to sit and perform the same hand movements as if you were holding a food-lure. Previously working with food in your hand as a lure has taught your puppy to watch your hand/lure movements, which have now become handsignals. Consequently, your pup will most likely follow the movement of your empty hand and sit. As soon as the pup sits, praise it profusely and quickly pull out a treat to give as a reward. After several trials, the word 'sit' becomes a verbal lure, since the puppy now understands the meaning of the word and sits when requested.

Always bear in mind, it is so much easier for a dog to respond to a handsignal than it is to respond to a verbal command. It is both natural and easy for dogs to observe and respond to body language such as ear movements, tail wags, body positions or in this case, human hand movements. If your puppy ever fails to respond to a verbal request, help the dog out, and immediately, give a handsignal. When working with food as a reward only, if necessary use another type of lure to facilitate the handsignal, such as a tennis ball, squeaky toy, chewtoy, food bowl, or anything the puppy values and will follow with its nose, eyes or ears.

Dinner time is another opportunity to practice. Prepare the pup's supper, and put the bowl on the counter. Give your puppy a hand signal and/or verbal request to sit and/or lie down, and when it does so, praise the pooch, and give it a piece of kibble from the bowl. If your pup does not respond - no big deal, put the bowl back on the counter, and try again later. Your pup will soon get the idea, because we are presenting it with a simple choice: sit for your supper or don't sit and don't get supper. Not only does the puppy become accustomed to working when the owner does not have food in the hand, but also it begins to learn the relevance of sitting when requested.

Remember, problems of control - when the dog's obedient performance becomes contingent on the owner having food in their hand - arise not so much because the dog knows the owner does not have food but because the owner knows there is no food and consequently has no confidence of success and so, does not even try. Just do it! Have the confidence to go cold turkey and work without food lures.

## Phasing Out Food Rewards

*1) Longer Sequences:* Whereas a single sit may be sufficient for a treat during the initial training session, surely it is not sufficient during subsequent sessions? We want the puppy to improve during the course of training, and so with each repetition, ask it to do a little more to receive an equivalent treat. For example, whereas a four-year-old child might justifiably be awarded a gold star for deducing that 2 + 2 = 4, surely a 40-year-old mathematics professor does not deserve a gold star for performing the same calculation. Neither does your dog. Be discerning with praise and rewards.

Once your puppydog sits eagerly and quickly for a treat, the next time ask it to do a little extra - to sit and then lie down before giving a slightly smaller treat. Then, ask it to sit, lie down and sit again for an even smaller treat. As training proceeds gradually and progressively increase the length of the training sequences, i.e., increase the number of responses necessary before giving smaller and smaller rewards. The hypothetical end-point of expecting more for less - the dog will perform an infinite number of commands for nothing.

Perform an extinction test - using food as a lure only, see how many doggy push-ups (alternating sits and downs) your pup will perform before giving up. For example, in their very first training session, Golden Retriever puppies (which I am convinced are whelped in sit-stays with dumbbells in their jaws) average 10 pushups (i.e., 20 responses) for the prospect of a single treat!

*2) Stay Delays:* In addition to increasing the number of responses, increase the length of time for which your pup has to respond before it receives its reward. Do not be in a hurry to stuff food in the dog's mouth. The longer you delay giving the food, the more attention you will command. Have your pup sit but delay giving the treat for just two seconds. During initial training, it is helpful to count the seconds as you praise the pup - "Good dog, one. Good dog, two" - before giving the treat. The next time, increase the stay-delay to three seconds before giving a treat, a chewtoy, or a bone and on subsequent trials, to five seconds, eight seconds and so on. If your puppy breaks the stay, there is no need for a reprimand even, since it doesn't yet understand what we mean. No big deal! Just repeat the request (plus handsignal) to sit, praise the pup as soon as it assumes the correct body position and start the count from zero again. Your puppy may Mickey-Mouse you around as much as it likes, but it will not receive the proffered treat until it stays in the prescribed position for the requisite amount of time. The pup will soon learn that 'staying put' is the quickest way to receive its reward. If, however, the pup fails three times in a row, discontinue this phase of the exercise - it is obviously too difficult. It is an important tactic in poker and training not to continue with a bad bet. However, it is vital to always end on a good note and so... sit down, calm down, and then try again, but using an easier body position (e.g. sit) and a shorter stay-delay (e.g. two seconds instead of eight).

Have competitions within the family to see who can hold on to the food lure for the longest time before giving it to the pup as a reward. Persevere. Soon the puppy will be performing bona fide three-minute sit-stays to receive a bona fide bone.

Repeat the above procedure for the down and stand positions. When practicing the sit/down/stand sequences, try to alternate a series of rapidly changing positions with variable length stay-delays in some positions. For example: Sit, Down-Stay (for 15 seconds), Sit, Stand, Down, Stand-Stay (for three seconds) and Sit-Stay (for 10 seconds).

*3) Differential Reinforcement:* Once the pup performs several responses for a single food reward, say for example, one reward for approximately every 10 responses or one reward for an average of 20 seconds of staying, when is the best time to give the food reward? Obviously, reward the better responses. The power of reward-training depends on only rewarding the pup for better responses and giving the best rewards for the best responses. As Gilbert and Sullivan might have said - Let the Reward fit the Deed. Grade each response, and reward the puppy accordingly. And be a strict judge. Insist on at least an above-average response before even considering rewarding your dog at all. Once your pup realizes only its better responses are reinforced, it will strive to do better.

*4) Life Rewards:* Once your dog can perform fairly long sequences per food reward, train it for short sessions in which it has to go 'cold turkey' on food rewards, and substitute them with other, more valuable rewards. For example, tell the dog to sit, lie-down and sit again, and then lavishly praise and pet the dog, and tell it to "Go Play," or "Fetch" a ball. If necessary, go back to using food as a lure to entice the dog to comply.

Food is a good reward when initially teaching the dog in the absence of distractions. However, in real life, unless you have a proverbial chow-hound, food loses its effectiveness. The owner wants the dog to sit and receive a food reward, but the dog would rather run and play. In these common life situations, the distractions themselves are the only effective rewards, i.e., life rewards. The deal is simple and one which your dog will quickly come to understand and appreciate: "If you sit, I'll let you go play. If you don't, I won't!" Relevancy training is an amazingly effective, easy and quick way to train.

## "OFF!" "TAKE IT" AND "THANK YOU"

These are three very useful commands which may be conveniently taught during your dog's dinner time. By hand-feeding the initial portion of your puppy's supper, it learns to take the food gently, and it may be taught the instructions " Off!" and "Take it!." "Off!" means don't touch the food unless told to "Take it!" Initially, the pup is trained that it will always eventually be allowed to take the food, so long as it doesn't touch for progressively increasing time intervals. By far, the best approach is to praise the cessation or absence of contact.

Give your pup a couple of pieces of kibble, then hold a third piece firmly between thumb and fingers. Let the pup sniff and lick, but say "Rover, Off." Allow the puppy to worry at the food treat in your hand for as long as it likes; eventually it will give up and withdraw its muzzle. The instant your pup breaks contact with your hand, say "Rover, take it" and offer the kibble by letting it fall into the palm of the hand, i.e., the pup has been rewarded for ceasing contact. Repeat this a couple of times. Next time, try for just a fraction of a second of non-contact before offering the food. Then delay offering the food for a full second after the pup breaks contact. On the next trial go for two seconds of non-contact. Praise your pup all the time it does not lick or paw, "Good dog, one; good dog, two" and then say "Rover, take it!" Now try for three seconds, then five and then eight and so forth. The pup develops confidence once it realizes "Off" does not mean it cannot touch the food at all, but if it waits for the "Take it" command, not only will it get the kibble but also plentiful praise and maybe even an additional tasty food treat into the bargain.

As soon as your pup learns not to touch the food for only a couple of seconds, you will proceed in leaps and bounds. The secret is to start with extremely short time periods, so that the puppy can succeed early on in training. If your pup noses or paws at the food during the forbidden time period, simply repeat the "Off!" request, and start the count from zero again. Your pup will learn that the quickest way to get the treat is by not touching it at all.

*1. "Off!"*        *2. "Take it"*
*Or, according to the Bitch 3rd Amendment to Hierarchical Law: "Take Both!"*

If ever the pup lunges or grabs, hold on tight to the kibble, loudly say "OUCH!," repeat "OFF!" in an injured but nonetheless authoritarian tone and start the count from zero once more. On no account, let the puppy get the food. Do not let the pup take the food roughly. There is no need to physically punish or even loudly reprimand the pup. It is only necessary to let your pup know it hurt you. But it is essential to let your pup know it hurt you. This time say "Gennnntly" in a soft, prolonged manner before telling the pup to take it. If the puppy ever nips or hurts you, hand feed its entire meal. You must resolve the problem right away. If you think it's bad now, wait until the pup becomes an adolescent.

To teach "Thank you," use an object of moderate value to the pup - a stick, a chewtoy or an old dry bone. When your puppy is chewing on its bone, say "Thank you," with an extremely tasty treat in one hand, take hold of the bone with the other hand, say "Take it" and

*Dart dutifully proffers Dad's slipper for a food reward*

offer the treat. Once the pup has eaten the treat, say "Off," proffer the bone and after a few seconds, tell the dog to "Take it." Repeat this several times before trying it with more valued objects, such as a juicy bone, the dog's food bowl or a paper tissue.

With the above exercises, dogs quickly develop confidence regarding human proximity around their valued objects. In fact, most dogs think this exercise is great. To indulge a little anthropomorphic license, perhaps they interpret "Thank you" to mean that the owner wants to hold their boring old bone and keep it safe, while the dog gets to munch on an extremely tasty treat.

"Off," "Take it," "Gently" and "Thank you" have numerous valuable applications. "Take it" encourages a fearful dog to take a food treat or toy from a stranger. "Gently!" instructs the dog how to take food from an unfamiliar child and how to play with the cat or a shy dog. Also, the "Off-Take it-Thank you" triad is a wonderful primer for later retrieval work.

On occasions, you may use "Off" to instruct the dog "Don't touch, period!" i.e., you say "Off" but do not then say "Take it." "Off" is useful to instruct a dog not to touch: the baby's diapers, the baby, the neighbor's bunny rabbit, a dead crow, fecal deposits of unknown denomination, a rattlesnake, a fearful dog or a large aggressive dog. It also warns a potential fighter not to touch the other dog.

You may use "Thank you" to expropriate articles already in the dog's possession, such as a box of tissues, a computer disk or the Sunday joint of meat. Say "Thank you," praise the dog and then instruct it to fetch a suitable chewtoy.

"Off" may be incorporated when using food lures in training to prevent the dog from slobbering over your mitts. For example, waggling a food treat to entice a pup to heel closely and attentively often over-stimulates the pup to make a play for the food. If you reprimand your puppy for nosing or grabbing food lures while heeling, you are also punishing the puppy for heeling. Soon your pup may learn that heeling is no fun. Instead, calmly say "Off," and then, excitedly waggle the treat to get an active heel.

# HOW TO TURN YOUR DOG OFF!

Learning "How to turn the little critter OFF" is one of the most important tricks of the trade. Living with a dog on Duracell starts to wear thin once you realizes your dog's speed and endurance are increasing with age. It becomes bearable only if your puppydog will settle down and be quiet for at least some of the time and especially at times of your choosing.

Establish the status quo right from the outset. Several times a day, put your pup on leash and have it settle down and be quiet for five minutes, half an hour or whatever. "Settle Down" means remain quietly in this spot, lying down comfortably. You may give your dog the option of stretching out, curling up, lying on its side or back or adopting the formal 'sphinx' down position. Your pup must be taught early that we have to have 'little quiet moments'. To remember to do this on a regular basis, it is a good idea to coordinate the exercise with owner-activities. For example, each family member should have the pup settle down next to them several times a day - each time he/she reads the newspaper, works on the computer, watches television, makes dinner eats dinner, or goes to bed. To make things easier, you may leash the dog or put it on a tie-down. Your pup may be restless and vocal at first, but within only a few days, it will soon get the picture.

Initially, have your puppy settle down right next to you, but later on, practice with your pup at a distance or in a different room. A useful trick is to incorporate the settle down request with a "Go to..." command and to tell the puppy to go to its mat (dog-bed, basket, kennel, crate, or tie-down etc.) and settle down. Tell your pup to go to its mat for example, and then lead it to the mat with a food treat, which the pup receives once it is lying down. Very young puppies learn place commands quickly and easily, and if the pup's basket, for example, is always kept in the same position, your puppy will learn the "Go to your basket" request in no time at all. While the pup remains put, periodically praise, pet or offer occasional food treats. If your pup tries to move, simply repeat the "Go to your mat" and "Settle down" requests, and this time, stay closer to the pup to control it.

Mats and crates are especially useful, since they are easily portable and can be a boon when traveling with the dog and staying at motels, the summer cabin or Granny's house. It is easy to throw down the dog's mat or set up its crate, and instruct the dog to settle down while unloading the car.

The settle down command renders even the most rambunctious and rumbustious little (or big) critter manageable at home. However, dogs are fine discriminators; they learn exactly what you teach them. If they have been taught to settle down at home, they will still act like maniacs at the park or in the vet's waiting room. Consequently, practice this exercise away from home.

When your puppy is old enough (completed its series of puppy shots) to go outdoors, train it to settle down on walks. Take along a newspaper or a gripping novel. At the corner of each block, tell the pup to settle down, and read a couple of pages before proceeding. Interspersing little quiet moments in an exciting walk is one of the best ways of teaching your puppy to settle down, no matter what the distraction. Moreover, each little quiet moment is reinforced by resuming the walk, i.e., you may now use the walk as a reward for good behavior many times over. (Otherwise, owners tend to use the walk as a reward only once, for unintentionally reinforcing the dog's

*Initially have your dogs settle down right next to you*

105

banana-like behavior when it sees its owner put on hat and coat or reach for the leash in preparation for a walk.) Similarly, during play sessions at home or in the park, periodically instruct your dog to settle down for a short time-out before resuming play.

The goal is not to spoil the puppy's fun by forcing it to settle down for hours on end but to frequently practice calming your dog when it is excited, so that you learn how to 'turn your dog off,' if and when necessary. If you can convince a distracted and playful puppy to settle down for just 30 seconds, you could easily keep the pup down for several minutes. The hard part is getting the pup to settle initially, not keeping it settled. Consequently, repeatedly ask your pup to settle down for many short periods within a single walk or play session. Integrating training is the secret to eager reliability.

## STAYS

The "Stay" request is different from "Settle Down." Whereas "Settle Down" means wait quietly in the designated spot but in any body position that is comfortable, "Stay" means remain in place and in the specific body position requested. Both "Settle Down" and the various "Stay" commands have many useful applications. "Settle Down" or "Wait" is generally used for longer periods of time at home, on picnics, in the car or in the veterinarian's waiting room. "Stay" is used for shorter periods. "Sit-stay" is useful when opening the front door, when getting out of your car, when greeting people. "Down-stay" is effective for controlling your dog around rambunctious children or fearful and aggressive dogs. "Stand-stay" and "Bang" (see Tricks) are essential when grooming the dog or during physical examinations in the veterinary clinic.

A good "Settle Down" command is the foundation for teaching specific stays. Once the pup has learned to stay put in a specific location, it is easier to teach it to stay in a specific body position. Also, when teaching the inhibitory "Off" command, you may already have discovered your pup voluntarily settled down or performed quite respectable stand-stays, sit-stays and down-stays of its own accord. Similarly, some family members have already enticed the pup to perform fairly lengthy and solid stays during the stay-delay exercise. The success of teaching "Stay" depends upon:

1) starting with very short stays, so your puppy may succeed from the outset and 2) frequently rewarding your pup while it remains in the appropriate position.

To teach stays, simply increase the length of time of the Stay-Delays discussed earlier. Start off with extremely short stays, so your pup may succeed and be rewarded for succeeding. Increase the length of the stays only very gradually. Do not push your pup to the point of failure. You will get frustrated, and your pup will probably be punished. This is not fair for either of you. Training is meant to be an enjoyable learning experience.

*With Phoenix positioned in front of the television during advertisements, it is easy to check for her head dropping during sit-stays*

Sadly though, some people do just about everything wrong when teaching stays. They command the puppy as if it were in boot camp, force it into position, stare at it menacingly whilst it remains in position, offering not a single word of thanks as they proceed to push the pup to the very precipice of failure, and then, when eventually and predictably, the poor puppy breaks its stay, it is reprimanded and physically forced back into position. For goodness sakes, if you're eager to punish something, go and punish a rock. But if you want to teach your dog to stay, let's do it in a fair and proper fashion.

Although your pup does not appear to be doing much when it stays, it is in fact inhibiting its movement for a long period of time, which is an utterly tremendous achievement for any young puppy. As such, your pup deserves a whole lot of praise and/or rewards for its effort. Although an inhibitory command for the dog, initial stay-training should be an active teaching process for the owner. In order to receive absolute attention from your pup, you must devote absolute attention towards the pup. To teach stays quickly, your pup requires complete surveillance and continual feedback - "Good Sit-Stay, Rover," conveying four bits of information: 1) praise, 2) the pup's name, 3) the specific body position and 4) the concept command - stay.

*1) "Good Dog"* - Periodic praise informs your pup so far so good. During initial training especially, it is important to regularly praise and reward the pup for getting it right. Consider, for example, a dog which breaks a stay after only 15 seconds. If you observed your dog's stay in silence, only to reprimand it for breaking, your dog will learn staying is a drag, because it is punished after 15 seconds of stay. If, however, you praise your dog every three seconds: at least 12 seconds of stay have been rewarded before gently reprimanding the dog for breaking the stay. Thus, your dog will learn that staying is good and breaking the stay is bad. Now, we're getting somewhere.

On their own, punishments are counterproductive - tending to de-stabilize stays and erode the dog's trust in the owner. On the other hand, each reward reinforces the specific stay position, as well as building the dog's confidence to accept and learn from occasional instructive reprimands.

Of course, with a young puppy, until it understands the meaning and the relevance of staying, it will not be reprimanded at all. Instead, just request the pup to sit again, and perform a couple of shorter stays (say six seconds and eight seconds) in an easier body position. Praise the pup all the time it stays, and reward it with a treat once it completes the short stays successfully. Then, try for a longer 15-second stay once more.

*2) "Rover"* - Using the puppy's name as a prefix for all puppy commands informs the pup the instruction was intended for Rover, not Fido and not Jamie. The pup has a name, and so let's use it: "Rover, Sit," "Rover, Down," "Rover, Sit-Stay," "Good Dog, Rover," "Good Sit-Stay Rover."

*3) "Sit"* - When teaching three or more stay positions, it is vital to repeat the specific position command, in this case, "Sit." Otherwise your pup may get confused. Breaking position but remaining in place or running to the owner, are both signs of a confused puppy which is still trying to please its owner. Similarly, breaking stays to run off to play with other dogs is also a sure-fire sign of a confused puppy, even though it is trying to please itself. Both of these confused puppies are insufficiently trained. Back to square one. Later in training, "Sit!" will be used as an instructive reprimand to counteract for broken stays.

*4) "Stay"* - Nearly everybody says the word "Stay," so enough said. Only, don't shout, and don't threaten. There is no need to command the pup, just politely request it to "Sit-stay" in a kind and reassuring voice. A well-trained dog willingly obeys whisper-requests. Of course, just because we ask the dog nicely does not mean to say it has the option of not complying. Once trained, if the dog breaks a stay, it will be reprimanded.

During stays, it is advisable to insist your puppy pay attention and watch you. However, if you do not pay attention, neither will your dog. And if your dog's attention is allowed to wander, so will your dog wander. Early stay-training is an active, exacting and exhausting endeavor for any trainer, so don't overdo it. Do lots of short stays, and then release your pup ("Puppy, Go Play") and relax. Better lots of short, successful stays with an eager puppy and a happy owner, than one long, boring, unsuccessful stay producing one tired and confused puppy and one mentally exhausted and very grumpy owner. Please note.

Once your pup has mastered 30-second sit- and down-stays, it is OK to gently reprimand the pup for making mistakes. However, make sure the reprimands are immediate and instructive. The instant your pup even thinks about breaking a sit-stay for example, tell it to "SSSIT!!! Staaaay" in a convincing tone with an emphatic sit-handsignal. This is an instructive reprimand, which conveys two vital bits of information in the shortest amount of time: the tone and increased volume lets the dog know it is about to make a mistake and the meaning of the word informs the dog what to do to make amends. Recommence praising your pup the instant it resumes a solid sit-stay. Speaking slowly and softly will tend to calm the dog and keep it in position.

The instructive "SIT!!! Stay" reprimand is by far the quickest way to get your pup back on track, should its attention wander. As such, it is the most humane reprimand. Reaching to jerk the dog's collar takes time. Walking back to the dog and reaching for its collar takes even more time. Also, the delayed punishment does not punish the dog for breaking the stay, instead it punishes the dog for remaining in place and allowing the owner to approach and grab its collar. The dog will not remain in place or allow someone to grab its collar for much longer. Now we have a dog which will neither stay in position nor remain in place, and it has become hand-shy as well. Bad news! Use instructive reprimands.

If, however, your pup does not sit immediately following an instructive reprimand: 1) Your Short-term Response - Quickly but gently, take hold of your pup's collar with both hands under its chin to gradually raise the pup's muzzle while peering down into its eyes. As soon as your pup looks up at you, it will sit. Please remember, once you have taken hold of your pup's collar, do not let go until your pup is back in the desired position. If your pup flinches, balks, ducks its head or runs away when you reach for its collar, disband stay-training for the time-being, and go back and perform the grab tests to immediately eliminate its hand-shyness. Why is the pup hand-shy? Try looking in the mirror. There's your answer. 2) Your Long-term Response - Go back and teach your dog both the meaning and relevance of the instruction "Sit."

*Solid sit-stays calm car-crazy canines*

If it is impossible to quickly take hold of your dog's collar because of the distance involved: 1) Your Short-term Response - Repeat the instructive reprimand while approaching your dog as quickly as possible - "Sit!... Sit!... Sit!", and praise the dog once it resumes the specific stay-position. 2) Your Long-term Response - For the next dozen or so stays, stay put. Do not leave your dog until it has mastered much longer stays in close proximity. If the dog has made a mistake and you try to repeat the same exercise, it is a good bet your dog will make the same mistake again. Do not set up yourself (and the dog) for failure. It is essential to further proof your dog before walking away again and expecting it to remain in position.

There are several factors which might prompt a dog to break a stay: 1) the length of the stay, 2) the level of distractions, 3) the owner moving away and 4) the owner returning. Both the length of the stays and the level of distraction may be increased with the owner in situ. Do not dream of leaving your dog until it can perform dead-dog stays for at least several minutes under extremely distracting circumstances.

Working extremely close to your dog (on leash as a precaution), employ the standard distractions: clapping your hands, tap dancing, bouncing tennis balls, placing food just out of the pup's reach, etc. Then, bring on the troops - family and friends and especially the kids - to run, skip, dance, squeak, scream, jump like frogs, do monster walks and otherwise act silly and have a good time. Then, practice near a children's playground, near a basketball court, around other animals and on busy sidewalks. Eventually, practice stays during doggy play sessions. Once stays are rock-solid with the owner 'up close and personal', it will be much easier to teach distance-stays.

Before leaving, get your dog used to your movement. Try circling your dog, make a few sudden and silly movements, jump, creep, kneel down, lie down and roll on your back. Make sure the dog is rock-steady. To walk away from your dog, initially only step back one pace, watch like a hawk, continually reassure and praise, "Good Sit-stay, Rover" and then, quickly return to your dog and give it a treat. Repeat this process many times over, progressively increasing the distance you leave. When working outside at distances greater than a couple of yards, either tie your dog's leash to a tree, have somebody else hold the leash or use a long line or a retractable flexi-leash. Whatever the arrangement, let the leash lie along the ground. The leash is a safety precaution to prevent the pup running to you or running away. The leash is not to restrain the pup - your brain and voice box can accomplish that.

## FOLLOWING

Right from the outset, teach your puppy the notion of following you around the house and garden and in other fenced or safe areas. The principle of following is simple in theory; the owner leads, and the puppy follows. However, in practice the 'following' exercise is a little more involved and extremely amusing to watch. During the first session, owners quickly realize that training is a two-way street. Furthermore, the owner-training skills of most puppies far exceed the puppy-training 'skills' of most owners. Characteristically, puppies demonstrate leadership, independence and improvisation, whereas the owners follow, wait, stand, stay and eventually try to catch up with the pup by pirouetting and walking backwards in circles.

The knack of getting your puppy to pay attention and follow is really quite simple. After giving a suitable command such as "Rover, Come Along," you should move away from your dog. Do not doddle around waiting for your dog to mobilize. Just Go! Motor! Boogie! The dog cannot follow you, if you don't go anywhere. If you hang around, aimlessly dithering and doodling, like a lettuce trying to take root, the pup will quickly get bored and wander off. Instead, walk fast and try to lose the pup, and you will find that it will stick to you like glue.

Whatever the pup's improvisations, alert your pup to its errant itinerary - "ROVER!!! Come Along," and quickly do the opposite. Do not change your intended direction to try to cover up for your pup's mistakes, or else it will never learn. Instead, accentuate the pup's mistakes a) if your pup slows down, 'give it some Welly' and sprint ahead, b) if your pup runs ahead, slow down, stop dead or turn around and walk quickly in the opposite direction, c) if your pup drifts left, turn right and accelerate and d) if your pup drifts right, turn left and speed up. Your puppy will soon learn to follow the leader, if

*Using a Frisbee to lure Oso
to follow on a right about turn*

*Using a Frisbee to lure dog to sit
by the handler's lefthand side*

you lead. After just a minute of active following, let the pup wander off and do its own thing for a while. Then, practice a little more following, then allow the pup to lead again and so forth.

A young pup will naturally follow its owner, as if there is an invisible social bungey-cord connecting person and pup. However, as the pup matures and becomes more confident, it has less need to remain close to its owner and will be more interested in investigating its surroundings. In a sense, you will be competing with the environment for your pup's attention. Practicing following in a setting which is unfamiliar to your pup (an enclosed tennis court or a friend's backyard) may revive your pup's inclination to stay close. You must train your pup to follow you by the time it is four and a half months old. The social bungey-cord breaks at five months of age, and after that, your adolescent dog's training skills, such as they are, take over.

Your young pup's off-leash attention can be substantially improved, if you run off and hide whenever your pup gets too far ahead or becomes overly preoccupied in some good sniffs. On realizing the owner is gone, most pups start to search frantically. Making strange noises in hiding increases the pup's desire to find the owner, and it helps a less confident pup locate the hiding place. Always keep a close eye on the pup, and call it should it wander too far in the wrong direction. Most pups soon learn to play the game of hide 'n seek and find their owners with little difficulty. Make sure to squeal with delight and praise the pup during the happy reunion. Other pups just have not got a clue. If you feel the pup has become too anxious, pop out from hiding and happily call the critter. With this fun game, puppies quickly develop the notion of keeping one eye or one ear on their owner at all times. It's as if the puppy learns that it can not afford to take its eyes off its silly owner even for a second without the owner becoming lost and making weird noises. Remember, play this game as early as possible around your house and garden. And certainly play this game in other safe outdoor areas before your puppy is four and a half months old. Unless previously trained to follow, after reaching adolescence, many dogs just do not care a wit whether their owners are in sight or on the moon.

# COME HERE

Call your puppy, "Rover, Come Here," praise it each step of the way, take hold of its collar and scratch its ear with one hand, and give it a treat with the other. It's as easy as that! Most puppies will approach their owners at the drop of a hat. Ordinarily, most three-month-old pups will approach virtually anything that has a pulse. A typical Labrador pup, for example, would run up and introduce itself to a fallen leaf.

Praising your pup is common human courtesy, in appreciation of the common canine courtesy of complying with your wishes. During early training, it is important to praise your pup all the time it approaches, because a young puppy may not come all the way to claim its reward. For example, if your pup comes 90% of the way and then becomes distracted, it will receive no reward for 90% of good recall. And 90% isn't that bad of a score. In fact, human nature being what it is, most likely the owner will become irritated and reprimand the pup when it arrives. Now, most puppies have a simple solution for this dilemma: "What if I just don't come at all!" The pup came most of the way when called, and it deserves to be rewarded most of the time. Do not think of a puppy-recall as an all-or-none response with the idea of reserving the reward for when the puppy gets to you. Instead, especially reward your puppy's first step towards you, and then continue to reward the pup all the time it approaches. Then, the next time, perhaps it will come 95% of the way. Hey! We're getting there!

At some time in its life, your puppy will: 1) start towards you but run off when it sees a distraction, 2) run off when you reach for its collar and 3) not even bother to come at all. Later on in training, we will reprimand the pup if it tries to run off, however, punishing the pup during early training would only decrease its tendency to come when called. Also, it would be unfair to reprimand the pup for doing something wrong, if we have not previously praised the pup for doing what is right. And so, for the meantime, praise your puppy all the time it is headed in your direction. If the pup does not come or if it reverses direction mid-recall, immediately get the pup's attention by shouting its name, and then quickly run away from the pup. Immediately begin praising your pup as soon as it is headed towards you once more.

Why give the pup a treat? Well, eventually, we want to consider a recall an all-or-none response and the food treat represents the icing on the cake - a special reward for your pup once it has completed the entire exercise. Since your pup receives the treat immediately after you have taken hold of its collar, in no time at all, it will eagerly anticipate you grabbing its collar. This in itself is an invaluable exercise. Repeatedly offering a food treat each time you take your pup's collar makes for an infinitely 'grabbable' dog. One day, you may need to grab your pup in an emergency. Should this happen, your pup will love it.

Puppies are easy to train to come when called. But that's not the point. Your mission, Mr. Phelps, is to get this pup thoroughly trained before it reaches adolescence and starts training you. A growing puppy adds numerous, new and annoying improvisations to the training arena as it embarks on a predictable developmental course through adolescence. One problem may lead to another. At first, the pup starts to duck its head, to balk and to flinch as the owner reaches for its collar. The pup is eager to approach the owner but does not want the owner to take its collar. This is just the tip of the iceberg, an important harbinger of more serious problems to come. Next, the pup will run up to the owner but will not come closer than arm's reach. Instead, it scurries around at a distance playing 'catch me, if you can'. And eventually, the pup does not bother to come at all. Why? Largely because, in the space of only two or three months, the owner has efficiently and effectively, albeit inadvertently, trained the pup not to come when called. How? The owner has unknowingly fallen prey to the very human foible of punishing the dog when it comes. Not only does the pup not want to approach the owner, it dare not.

Training a dog not to come when called does not necessarily entail reprimands or physical punishments. Luckily, few people would do something that silly. Unfortunately, some do. Some owners call the dog to 'express disapproval' if, for example, they encounter a wet spot in the rug or the confettied remains of a telephone directory. It doesn't take the brains of Einstein for a dog to learn when its owner calls with maniacal overtones, it is seldom in the dog's best interests to go and see what's up. Usually though, owners punish their dog for coming when called in more insidious and pernicious ways. There are two common scenarios.

1. The owner calls when the puppy is having a fine old time playing in the park or sniffing in the yard. The puppy obediently and trustingly bundles up to its owner, who snaps on the leash and takes it home or brings the dog indoors. Now, just a couple of canine neurons are more than sufficient for the pup to put two and two together and realize "Puppy Come Here" signals the end of an otherwise extremely enjoyable play session. Hence the pup learns whereas it is fine to periodically check in and visit the owner most of the time when playing off-leash, it must avoid its owner at all costs should it hear the dreaded words, "Puppy Come Here."

2. The puppy is contentedly sacked-out, snoozing on the rug in front of a blazing fire, and the owner says, "Puppy Come Here." The puppy interrupts its peaceful slumber to see what the owner wants, and the owner picks it up and puts it in the kitchen or shoos it outside into the cold before leaving for work. The pup quickly learns that approaching the owner at home when they say "Puppy Come Here" usually heralds eight hours of excruciating boredom and confinement to the kitchen or a whole day sitting on the porch in the freezing rain.

NEVER call your dog to punish it! If for example your dog soiled the house in your absence, it's too late for punishment now. Your dog cannot possibly associate the delayed punishment with the crime, but it will definitely associate the punishment with approaching its owner, i.e., you! Just put your dog outside while you clean up the mess. And in the future, until you have housetrained your dog, don't let it have the run of the house when you are not at home. If you do call your dog and punish it, not only will you still have to housetrain your dog, but also you will have to repair your dog's damaged confidence and retrain it to come when called.

NEVER use "Come Here" as a control-command to get the dog's attention to stop it playing or investigating, until you have practiced and perfected reliable, integrated recalls. Until then, use "Sit" or

"Down" - much simpler emergency control commands - and then say "Come Here" once you know you have the dog's attention (because it is sitting). A reliable recall is one of the most difficult commands to maintain, whereas "Sit" and "Down" are the two easiest.

NEVER call your dog to confine it. Instead use a place-command, such as "Go to your Crate," "Go to your Mat" or "Outside."

## COMMAND LEVELS

"Settle Down" (remain quietly and comfortably in this spot), "Come Along" (follow), "Come Here" (approach and allow trainer to take your collar) and "Walk On" (walk on-leash without pulling but sniff and pee at will) are all lower-level informal commands for casual use around the home and on walks. "Stay" (remain put in designated body position), "Come" (come here and sit facing trainer) and "Heel" (walk by trainer's side and sit when trainer stops) are middle-level formal commands, which offer the owner a more precise control over the dog's activity and body position.

The dog learns the basic command concept with a fair degree of reliability when teaching low-level, fairly flexible informal commands. The dog learns absolute reliability when performing middle-level formal commands, usually with a fair degree of style. Once the dog is reliable and will always do what you ask, it is time to teach the dog to perform with pizzazz, panache and ultra-precision. A reliable off-leash performance is a wonderful and essential foundation for enrolling in a class which teaches competitive obedience. Try it - You'll enjoy it. Handlers, who train for working trials and/or competitive obedience, would teach yet another family of commands - top-level patterned commands, affording ultra-precise, reliable control over the dog.

Informal commands form the foundation for reliable formal commands. Later on in training, you will learn how to alternate between the two levels. For example, letting the dog walk on-leash around the block but periodically calling it to heel when crossing the street and then, resuming to informal control when the potential danger has passed.

# COME AND SIT

To train your pup to come and sit: 1) Call your pup, "Rover Come," and praise it all the time it approaches. Hold out a food treat to focus your pup's attention, and when your pup is just two or three pup-lengths away, 2) instruct it to "Sit" followed by the lure-handsignal to sit. 3) Do not touch your pup until it is sitting. (Unless of course, it is about to bolt. In which case, it is prudent to prevent things going from bad to worse by quickly and gently taking hold of its collar.) As soon as your pup sits, 4) take hold of its collar, praise and pet the pup and give it the food lure as a reward. Let's go through these four steps one at a time:

*1) Why call the pup?* Pretty obvious! You are here and the pup's there. The whole point of the exercise is for pup and owner to rendezvous at the owner's present location.

*2) Why ask the pup to sit when it comes?* Normally, we want the pup to come and stick around for a while. We do not want the pup to come and trample us like third base heading for home, so we want the pup under control. Down-stay would be overkill - especially for large dogs, and stand-stay would be too unstable. Sit is ideal.

*3) Why not touch the dog until it sits?* We do not want to touch the dog for a variety of reasons.

    a) The use of physical prompts delays the ultimate learning process of establishing off-leash, distance control. We want the dog to learn the meaning of words and handsignals, not the meaning of touches. Using physical prompts, training becomes a longer and more involved two-step process. Certainly, the dog quickly learns to sit when touched on the collar or pushed on the rump, but it takes considerably longer for the dog to learn to sit when we say "Rover, Sit." It is quicker to teach the pup the meaning of the word "Sit" from the outset, in just one step.

    b) There are many times when it is not possible to touch the dog. What if the owner's hands are full? Carrying a child, or bags of groceries? Or, if the pup comes most of the way but stops just short of arm's reach? Without verbal control, the owner will not be able to control the pup.

c) A well-socialized puppy is centripetally attracted towards its owner and needs to periodically check in to get another confidence booster before embarking on another exciting foray into the great unknown. As soon as the owner touches the pup, it no longer feels insecure and is ready to shoot off and explore once more.

d) Whereas a good trainer can use physical prompts to great effect for guiding a pup into desired body positions, with a novice teacher and/or a slow-learning pup, physical prompts tend to degenerate into force, and the poor pup is pushed and pulled into position. With forceful training methods, the pup understandably develops a strong antipathy towards training in general and towards human hands in particular.

e) All family members have to learn to control the dog, but many of them, e.g., children, can neither effectively guide the dog into position, nor can they force it to comply. It is prudent to employ a training method which all family members can master.

*4) Why take the pup's collar when it arrives?* The whole point of the exercise is to call the pup (which is off-leash) and get it under control. What better control than to have firm hold of your dog's collar? Customarily, taking hold of the collar during practice runs makes it easy to do during an emergency. So many puppies will

*Using a tug toy to lure Phoenix to come…*

approach their owners enthusiastically, only to bolt the instant they see that human hand reaching out to grab them. The dog has developed grabitis because the human hand has been up to no good in the past. Thus, we take hold of the collar and then, give the pup a food treat. In no time at all, the pup is eager to come and sit, and just cannot wait for the owner to grab its collar.

Before tagging a 'sit' onto the end of a recall, make sure that your dog's position commands are up to scratch. Until such time as your puppy sits reliably and immediately whenever asked, practice the two commands separately, i.e., position sequences at one time, and recalls without sits ("Come Here") at other times. It is an utter and diabolic disaster in training whenever an enthusiastic recall is followed by a sloppy sit, a slow sit or by no sit at all, prompting the owner to reprimand the dog for its imperfect sit and/or to force the dog to sit. Not only has the owner punished the dog for its below par or absent sit, but also the owner has punished the dog for coming when called. Do you think the pup likes to go to its owner to get grief? No, of course not. And the dog has a simple solution: not to come at all. Poor sits will destroy recalls in short order. Also, they destroy heeling. If your pup does not yet sit quickly, reliably (and precisely), do not ask it to sit after a recall or whilst heeling.

*...and sit*

## HEELING OFF-LEASH

It is important for the family to agree to heel the pup on one side. It is bad news for the pup to cross over from one side to the other. Eventually, you will tread on it causing injury, or you will trip over the pup and injure yourself. Changing sides is also dangerous on-leash. If the pup circles its owner, the leash might wrap around the owner's legs, and the owner hits the dirt like a hog-tied heifer. Most trainers teach people to heel dogs on the left, because this is required in most obedience competitions. However, if for some reason you want to heel the dog on the right, that's fine, just reverse the following instructions.

For a single heeling-sequence: 1) Get your pup to sit facing forwards by your left side by saying "Rover, Heel-Sit" and using a food-lure handsignal with the right hand to accurately position the pup. It's helpful at least to start with both owner and dog facing forwards. Hold food treats in both hands. One piece in the right hand for the next sit signal and the rest in the left hand to heel the pup. 2) Bait your puppy and peak its interest by waggling the left hand in front of its nose, say "Rover, Heel" and move your left hand from left to right in front of the pup's nose (heel signal) and quickly take three huge steps forwards. 3) After saying "Rover Sit," slow down, motion sit with the right hand and then stand still and offer a food treat once your pup has sat by your left side. When stopping, try to remain facing forwards and give the sit signal in front of the pup's nose with your right arm crossing in front of your body. Thus, the pup will come to sit by the owner's left side, facing forwards and all ready for the next heeling sequence.

After saying "Rover, Heel," move off briskly. If you want some snappy heeling, your pup has to learn that the word "Heel" means action. Don't dilly dally around. Keep your pup on its toes. Let's be disciples of digitigrade; no time for plantigrade plodders here! Should your puppy attempt to improvise on the heeling pattern, as with "Following" do the opposite and do it quickly. Accentuate your pup's mistakes, and make the puppy hustle to correct itself.

Sometimes, work with food as a lure only, but do not give it as a reward. Praise or pet your dog instead. At other times, keep the food in your shirt pocket as occasional rewards for especially good heeling sequences, and use lure/hand movements with empty hands (hand signals) or maybe use other lures, such as a tennis ball, or squeaky toy. At yet other times, keep the food in your pocket and don't use it at all; instead use different lures (hands, tennis ball) and different rewards (praise, petting, "Go Play," "Go Fetch" etc.). During initial training with most puppydogs, food is the very best choice of training lures and rewards. However, you want to phase out the use of food as soon as possible.

Before heeling anywhere, it is vital the pup can sit at the drop of a hat. If the pup does not yet sit quickly and eagerly, heeling will become a drag for both owner and dog. Heeling a poor sitter is frequently interspersed with frustrating moments, when the owner reprimands the dog for not sitting. However, with prompt and reliable sits, off-leash heeling may be taught via a simple sequential process, with the pup assuming a controlled heel-sit position each time the owner stops between each sequence. Active, precise heeling requires a lot of attention and mental energy; the heel-sit is the recovery period. In addition, the heel-sit is the owner's emergency control command. Whenever things begin to drift out of control, immediately instruct your dog to "Sit." Good sitting is essential for good heeling.

*Initially hold a toy or food lure to position your dog by your side*

# Heeling Sequences

Always think of heeling in sequences: 'three steps heeling and then, puppy-sit and owner-relax'. Phew! Take another treat in the right hand and then repeat the sequence. Always start each sequence with your dog in the exact heel-sit position. There is no sense in starting with the dog out of position and then, further complicating the issue with motion. Things will only go from bad to worse. If your pup is facing sideways or looking backwards, say "Rover, Heel-Sit" and reposition the dog using the food lure in the right hand before moving off in the heel.

Until it is possible to string together several short heeling sequences, always heel in a dead straight line. Instead of turning when in motion, come to a stop, instruct the dog to "Heel-Sit," turn in place and reposition the dog with the lure in the right hand, i.e., to get your dog to perform a bunny-hop sit-adjustment in place, so that you and the dog are both facing in the new direction.

# Heeling Strategies

There are two basic heeling strategies depending on your dog's size, speed, and frame of mind: 1) rapid heel-sit sequences for small and/or fast dogs and 2) long straight-aways with infrequent sits for large lumbering dogs. Rapid-fire, multiple heel-sit sequences are also useful for a lackadaisical dog - to blow the cobwebs out of the dog's brain when it is goofing around and not paying much attention.

*1) The Paquita Principle* - The biggest problem with little dogs is speed; the dog is everywhere and then some. Initially, speed works against training. However, once the speed has been marshaled and brought under control, little dogs make for flashy obedience. With small and/or fast dogs, do a series of one-step heeling sequences before trying to take two steps. Some dogs are so fast that they have vaporized before the second step. And so, don't try to heel for two steps until you can heel for one. Once your dog can perform a rapid-fire, staccato sequence of several one-step heels and sits in succession, try some two-step heeling sequences, then three-step sequences and so on. In no time at all, long, straight-away heels will be a piece of cake.

When heeling little dogs in this fashion, initially it will be necessary to bend the knees and walk Groucho-style to accurately lure the pup with the left hand. As heeling progresses and you are taking longer straight-aways, stand up and walk quickly -the faster you move, the easier it is. A pup with little legs will have to walk a straight line to keep up. It will only be necessary to bend down when giving the signal to sit or to occasionally gather the pup's attention during mid heel. Otherwise, after giving the heel-signal, the left hand may be held comfortably at waist level, which encourages the puppy to look up. To further entice your pup to look up and pay attention, you might want to try using human food as lures and rewards, and keep it in your mouth, periodically moving your left hand from mouth (to get a treat) to the pup's nose (to lure and/or reward).

A 30-inch length of rigid plastic 1" diameter pipe is a wonderful training aid for little dogs. After priming your puppy by dropping several pieces of dinner kibble down the tube, it is possible to manipulate the bottom of the pipe to precisely position your pup when heeling. Tape a bent spoon to the bottom of the pipe (to catch the kibble), teach your pup "Off" and the positioning pipe is even more effective. Moreover, by threading the puppies leash through the pipe is it possible to construct a 'solid-lead'. Thus, the pup's leash only has a couple of inches free play at the bottom of the pipe. The puppy is quite comfortable. It is accurately positioned by your side, and it can not get underfoot.

*2) Long Straight-aways* - Generally, when heeling big dogs - the sack o' potato, moose-like breeds, it is not wise to include too many sits. Large dogs seldom derive much pleasure from bobbing up and down like a yo-yo. With large dogs, long straight-aways are the name of the game. It is imperative to start with your moose pointed in the intended direction, and then instruct and/or signal it to heel and off you go - QUICKLY - like a bullet out of a gun - in a dead-straight line for at least 30 feet before slowing down to sit your dog. During the first few heels, many owners will get a good 10 feet away before the pup even moves, and then, whooooshhh! - the moose catapults to heel position. The pup learns: "Wow! When she says "Heel," she's gone! Will I have to watch her!" If you always move off quickly, your pup will begin to move off smartly, such that when it comes time to heel at normal speeds, your puppy will be right there glued to your left side with Velcro shoulder pads.

Motel hallways are some of the best places to practice heeling (and recalls). Drive to a motel that accepts pets. (There is always convenient parking.) Go in the side entrance and up to the second floor, and off you go. No freezing cold in Omaha, no drizzle in Seattle and no blazing sun in Phoenix. Just a long straight hallway with fire-doors (safe), and carpets (good traction) and environmental control (comfort). If anyone sees you, just say "Sorry, wrong floor."

Large dogs especially need lots and lots and lots of encouragement when heeling. Without sufficient praise, maintaining an enthusiastic and speedy response becomes progressively harder as the dog gets older. Always try to walk as quickly as possible. It is vital to instill the notion of speed into the dog before we introduce on-leash heeling. With most dogs, ill-administered leash corrections tend to slow the dog down even more - the more you pull and jerk, the more the dog resists.

## Three Gears of Heeling

Varying speed or 'changing gears' is one of the best ways to keep the puppy's attention. If your pup feels that nothing much is happening and you are not going anywhere in particular, it will quickly get bored and wander off. Think of heeling in three gears: slow, normal and fast. Make lightning gear changes, but at first, inform the pup when you are about to change. Before changing up, say "Hustle" or "Quickly" (the particular word does not matter to the puppy - your choice), and rapidly accelerate from slow to normal, from normal to fast or directly turbo-change from funeral-slow to Warp Factor 9. Similarly when changing down, say "Steady" and instantly decelerate from fast to normal, from normal to slow or from fast to slow. Your pup will soon anticipate your change of speed as it learns that "Hustle" means you are about to gun it and "Steady" means you are about to hit the brakes.

In no time at all, "Hustle" prompts your puppy to speed up and "Steady" causes it to slow down. Wonderful! When walking at the same pace,

*Activate your dog
before turning right*

*Lead it round the turn*

*Speed off in the straight-away*

"Hustle" and "Steady" now become wonderful corrections for pups that are lagging or forging. These instructive reprimands allow the owner to correct the dog's improvisations when heeling off-leash, and they remove the need for much pulling and jerking during on-leash heeling. Both commands facilitate negotiating turns during heeling. Additionally, "Hustle" is a marvelous instructive reprimand to speed up slug-like recalls.

## Turns

When turning to the left or on left-about-turns, say "Steady," place the palm of your left hand in front of your pup's nose and move it backwards, so that your puppydog's head is slightly behind your left knee before you turn. Otherwise, if the pup is too far ahead when turning left, either you will bump into the pup, or it will scoot forwards and end up on your right side after the turn.

When turning to the right or on right-about-turns, say "Hustle," waggle the left hand in front of the pup's nose to position your puppy's head in front of your left knee before making the right turn. Otherwise, when you turn right, a smart pup or a lazy pup will take the shortcut behind you to end up on your right side after the turn.

## WALKING ON-LEASH

Forging ahead is the biggest problem when walking adolescent dogs on-leash. Dogs pull on leash for a variety of reasons. Many adolescent dogs pull on-leash, because they were allowed to pull as puppies. Once the leash is tightened, your dog no longer has to pay attention to you, since it has a taut telegraph wire through which it may sense your every move and even your very intentions, thus freeing its nose, ears and eyes to 'scope the 'hood. Also, it would appear that pulling on leash is intrinsically enjoyable and self-reinforcing for many dogs. It is as if most dogs view a trip to post a letter at Shattuck and Vine as a work-out for the Iditarod. Whatever the reason, leash-pulling is usually unacceptable and often dangerous. Once the leash is tightened, you can no longer control your dog - a principle of elementary physics.

It is considerably easier and smarter to first practice all of these exercises with the young puppy on-leash indoors. Also, to have a simple rule that no one, that is NO ONE, is allowed to walk the pup on-leash outdoors, not even a single step, unless they can walk the puppydog without it pulling. It is utterly unfair to let a puppy develop a leash-pulling habit, knowing full well it will be punished for the same habit as an adolescent. It is so much easier to establish an acceptable status quo from the outset. Just bear in mind, the dog weight-pulling record is in the region of 10,000lbs, i.e., in just a few months time, your average dog will have the power to pull the entire Cowboys' defensive line backwards. From the getgo, NEVER permit leash-pulling to get going.

Using a leash to walk the puppy is necessary as a safety precaution, and leashing the dog is mandatory when leash laws are in effect. However, once a novice owner and an adolescent dog are connected with a leash, the dog will pull. And to stop the dog from pulling, usually (but not always) the owner pulls back, i.e., the owner jerks the leash. Most owners find this unpleasant. And it is not much fun for dogs either. Since we do not want the dog to associate walking and heeling with numerous physical leash corrections, we must first make sure the dog can stand calmly on-leash before further exciting the dog by moving.

## Red Light - Green Light

Firstly, before even considering leash training, make sure that you can get your pup to follow you around the house and garden and that it will happily sit-stay in front of you for a good 30 seconds. Surely you would want to check to see that your puppy feels good about following and staying close before you physically restrain its activity with a leash. After all, leash-pulling does advertise the fact your dog wants to get away from you. So, give your dog a reason to stick around. Lighten up, brighten up and maybe offer the dog an occasional kind word, pat or treat.

Secondly, before going anywhere, let's make sure that your dog knows how to stand around on-leash without pulling. Initially, let's practice indoors because: 1) you may start training well before your pup has completed its shots, 2) there are fewer distractions and 3) it avoids the embarrassment of making a spectacle of oneself on the street.

Put your pup on leash. Firmly grasp the end loop with both hands held close to your body. Stand perfectly still, and pay absolute attention to your pup, but ignore all antics at the other end of the leash. Eventually, your pup will sit or lie down. Yes, it will. Just be patient and wait and see. When it does so, immediately say "Good dog," offer a treat, say "Let's Go," take one step forwards and then stand still again. Be prepared; taking a single step will energize your pup, and it will lunge with vengeance. Again, ignore the puppy's antics, and wait until it sits once more. Then, reward your dog, take another step and stand still again. With successive trials, have your dog sit for progressively longer periods before praising it and taking another step. Once it is possible to alternate single steps with standstills without the pup pulling, try taking two steps at a time before standing still. Then try three steps, four steps and so on. As with off-leash heeling, think of it in short sequences. Once the sequences have expanded to six or seven steps, you are now walking your pup on-leash without it pulling, and it will sit automatically by your side whenever you stop. If your puppy ever tightens the leash when you are walking, immediately stand still and wait for it to sit again before moving on.

Basically, this technique is a variation of 'red light - green light,' and as with all effective training methods, you have duped your puppy into believing that it is training you. Perhaps your canine companion muses, "My owners are so easy to train. Just barely tighten the leash, and they stand stay. Sit down, and they move ahead." Your dog's happy, and so are you.

## Walking Sequences

Practice walking your pup on-leash around the house and garden, interspersed with many stops. Say "Rover, Let's Go" or "Come Along" each time before you walk (again, the precise words do not matter - you choose), and instruct the pup to "Sit" each time you stop. When your puppy is old enough to walk on the sidewalks, first try walking in the hallway with the front door open, then practice leaving and entering the house. Dogs commonly tend to lunge at doorways, and so this is worth a little extra special practice. Leave and return several times in a row, and soon your pup will be picture perfect. Have your puppy sit both before and after going through the door. Then, walk back and forth in front of the house. Walk and standstill in sequences, and keep repeating the sequences over and over. Remember, it is always the hardest the first time you try. If the dog pulls, say "Steady" and stand still. Once the pup sits, go back and repeat the sequence. It will be much easier the next time.

Now, you are ready for several laps round the block. Much like horses, dogs will tend to forge when leaving home but lag when coming back. If the puppy pulls on the way out, say "Steady," about turn, and frog-march the pup back home and start again. The first trip around the block may take a long time, but the second and third laps are progressively easier, and thereafter, it's a breeze.

Basically, dogs pull because: 1) pulling is enjoyable, 2) the owner lets the dog pull and 3) the owner follows. The same basic principles for teaching dogs to follow off-leash may be used to teach a dog to walk on-leash. Hold the leash with both hands close to the left side of your body, so as to give the puppy just a couple of inches of slack, then start walking and keep walking. Whatever the puppy does to improvise on your intended direction, do the opposite. If the puppy lunges ahead, just do a smooth right-about turn and head off in the opposite direction. If the puppy pulls left, turn right. If the puppy

*Remember to use hand signals to focus your dog's attention*

drifts right behind you, turn left. If the puppy drifts right in front of you, speed up to cut-off the pup, and then turn left in front of it. If the puppy slows down to sniff or pee, that's fine - this is usually the reason we are walking the dog - slow down and wait for the pup. Of course, if you want your pup to come along, say "Come Along" and/or "Hustle," and off you go. This method works well when practiced at home with young puppies or in the park with older puppies, adolescent and adult dogs.

## Pulling On Cue

Some owners might consider allowing the dog to pull when convenient. Look, if the dog has got a bee in its bonnet about pulling, if pulling on-leash is such a thrill, why be a killjoy? Why not let the draught doggie pull at acceptable times? Only of course, when given the OK by the owner - "Rover, Pull," "Mush," "Hike" or whatever. Personally, I appreciate Phoenix's tractor beam up the Rose Walk steps and the "Pull" command is a boon when we harness her to our sled in the Sierra: "Phoenie, Pull!" Whoooshhhhh. Yea! Way to go!

## HEELING ON-LEASH

Heeling a dog on-leash offers the most controlled manner of walking with a dog. It is most useful when cruising crowded sidewalks or when other dogs and animals are around. For many dogs, unfortunately, on-leash heeling is the most unpleasant command (having the highest correction/command ratio of any other obedience instruction), so much so, that heeling around the block becomes a drag in both senses of the word. The dog must think there is a jerk at both ends of the leash.

Sadly, some trainers teach on-leash heeling using non-specific (non-instructive) leash-corrections from the outset. Certainly, in some situations, a leash-correction is ideal for enforcing an already learned command, but it has absolutely no place in teaching either the meaning or the relevance of our instructions. Incessant, non-instructive physical corrections destroy the dog's spirit. Many dogs become dejected the instant they hear the instruction "Heel." And the owner wonders why? And then, the owner has to go to a motivational training workshop to re-motivate a dog, which was more than adequately motivated before they started training!

To start heeling instruction by enforcing compliance on-leash using physical prompts and punishments takes much longer and tends to produce a Jekyll and Hyde performance. The dog may act like a perfect angel on-leash, but as soon as the leash is removed, the dog is history. The dog quickly learns that its owner can not control it when out of arm's reach.

For these and other reasons, we teach heeling on-leash as the last of five progressive steps: 1) Following off-leash, 2) Heeling off-leash, 3) Standing on-leash, 4) Walking on-leash and finally 5) Heeling on-leash.

Once your dog has mastered the principles of following and understands the specific "Hustle," "Steady" and "Heel-Sit" commands and once it has learned not to pull when standing or walking on-leash, then off-leash heeling may be taught with nary a leash correction. Moreover, teaching dogs to heel off-leash from the outset teaches owners to control their dog using brain instead of brawn, since there is no opportunity to push and pull the dog around under the guise of training. Initial off-leash heeling also produces a more reliable dog, at which point it is a simple matter to slip on a leash and fine-tune heeling, once the dog already understands the basic underlying principles off-leash.

Start with your pup in a sit-stay by your left side. Hold the leash with the left hand, so that it loosely dangles a couple of inches below the point where it attaches to the pup's collar and slip your right hand through the end loop, holding any excess leash tidily bunched up in this hand. Keep both hands on the leash at all times. As with off-leash heeling, have a bunch of treats in the left hand (if necessary) to precisely guide the pup, and have one treat in the right hand for the sit signal. Say "Rover, Heel" and/or give a heel-signal (without letting go of the leash) by moving your left hand from left to right in front of the pup's nose, so that your left arm comes to rest comfortably in front of your waist and off you go. Quickly! The faster you walk, the easier it is. If the puppy lags or becomes distracted, quickly waggle the left hand in front of its nose, and then bring it back to lie in front of your waist.

Each time before stopping, slow down, say "Rover, Sit," give a sit-signal with your right hand (still attached to the end of the leash) across the front of your body and in front of the pup's nose and then, come to a halt with the pup sitting in heel position. In time, your puppy will learn to anticipate the sit signal and will sit automatically each time you slow down to stop. If necessary, use food as both a lure and a reward, and phase it out as before.

Your puppy may gradually lose attention during long and/or slow straight-away heels. To keep the pup on its toes, continually and randomly change pace and direction. Successive changes of pace are by far the best. Run up and down through the three-gears of heeling. This is convenient because, for the most part, it is difficult and sometimes dangerous to make a sudden turn when walking along the sidewalk - you'll probably end up in the street, in a neighbor's front yard or up a tree someplace. Open spaces are the place to practice multiple right- left- and about-turns. Happy heeling!

REMEMBER, if ever you feel it is necessary to correct your dog either 1) your dog did not understand the meaning of your instructions (possible) and/or 2) your dog did not understand the relevance of your instructions (highly probable). Every correction, reprimand or punishment is a blatant advertisement that your dog is not yet adequately trained. Do yourself and your dog a favor: go back and retrain your dog.

## Integrating Heeling into Walks

On-leash heeling is precise and controlled. However, that is not to say we necessarily want to heel the puppy all the way around the block. "Hey! What about the sniffs and pees?" Let's consider the dog's very heart and soul, and think about a little olfactory gratification here and there. The walk, after all, is meant to be enjoyable - one of the biggest treats of the day for owner and dog. We do not need to be on military alert all of the time. Too much regimental heeling and your dog will become bored, frustrated and distracted, and the quality of heeling will eventually deteriorate. To maintain high-level, snappy heeling when required, 20:1 is a good walking-to-heeling ratio.

When walking, the dog is allowed to dally, to dawdle, to sniff and investigate to its heart's content. The only proviso being that it must not tighten the leash. When heeling, the dog must perform an exact and snazzy choreography dictated by its owner. The dog must walk precisely by its owner's side, turn when its owner turns and sit when its owner stops. When heeling, the dog should not be allowed to sniff or look around; it must pay attention. Certainly, the dog should not eliminate. (Most elimination is best done in the backyard or at least close to home, with a walk offered as the grand prize for the cutting-edge in canine eliminatory etiquette). Heeling is a formal control command used, for example, when crossing the street. We hardly want a dog to decide to defecate when hurry-heeling across a street just before the lights are about to change.

To obtain absolute attention from the dog, the owner must devote absolute attention to the dog. And this is tiring. Most people cannot heel their dog effectively for more than a couple of minutes at the most. Consequently, integrate several short, active and precise heeling sequences into a long, luxurious and enjoyable walk. Start with a 30-second, extremely active heeling sequence to blow the cobwebs out of the dog's cerebrum, and then walk for three minutes, heel for five seconds and walk for one minute, heel for 10 seconds and walk for two minutes and so on. A good rule of thumb is to walk along the sidewalk and to heel when crossing streets or passing pedestrians, dogs or other animals.

## NOT COMING WHEN CALLED

When dogs fail to come when called their behavior falls into one of two categories: active or passive disobedience. With passive disobedience, the dog doesn't come and it isn't doing much else besides. Instead it simply stands, sits or lies down and watches its owner call. Either the dog is apprehensive of approaching (a major temperament emergency), or it fails to see the relevance of the owner's request and simply can not be bothered (a minor training emergency). With active disobedience, however, not only does the dog not come, but also, it has a darn good time not coming. This is a major training emergency.

## Apprehensiveness

If your dog is apprehensive of coming when called, there is only one reason... You! Take yet another look in the mirror. Your dog is afraid of you or of what you have done to it in the past - probably intentionally punishing the dog for coming when called. Whatever the reason, just solve the problem right away. Even though apprehensiveness is a dire temperament emergency, take your time. Get sweet and get small. Keep backing up and calling the dog, tossing food treats if necessary. Once the dog approaches to take food from your hand, practice the 'grab tests'. Build your dog's confidence, and its so-called obedience problem will disappear.

## Lack of Relevance

Your dog understands what you want it to do but it just does not see the point. Also, your dog may be tired, bored, or lethargic. For large dogs especially, it is a big deal to get up and lumber towards the owner. When they get there, it better be worthwhile. Well, it wasn't! And now the dog is on strike. The dog came when called many times before, but nothing ever happened. Perhaps the owner even practiced recalls to the point of utter boredom. This problem is so common; this is what training is all about. I would say that 95% of a successful training program should comprise not just teaching dogs what we want them to do but teaching them why they should do it! The solution is to revamp the relevancy training program (see sections on Play Recalls and Life Rewards).

If your dog does not come, give it a reason to come. Tell it to "Hustle," back up quickly and cause some kind of disturbance - rattle the furniture, bang on the door, kick the dog's food bowl or drop to the ground, kick you feet in the air and let out an eerie maniacal wail. The idea is to get your dog's attention, and so do something attention-getting. Whatever you do though, eventually your dog will come. When it does, on no account punish or reprimand the dog. Don't even let on that you are grumpy. Instead, let your dog know what it missed by not getting there earlier. Waggle an extremely tasty treat in front of the dog's nose, tease the dog with the treat and then give it to another dog, or even eat it yourself. Or show the dog its empty food bowl and say, "Oh dear, dindins all gone!" Or drop the dog's leash on the floor and lament, "Deary, deary me, slow-poke snail-pooch missed his walky, walky, walkies." The dog will soon grasp the relevance of coming when called.

Lazy dogs often refuse to come when called because they know the owner will eventually come to them. Many owners start towards the dog the instant they call it. Perhaps the owner has no confidence the dog will come and so, completes the recall himself with food treat in hand, as if auditioning as a waiter. Never go back to the dog. Move away from it, and make it come to you. This advice, of course, refers to a dog that is not coming but is not doing much else. If, however, your dog is sniffing, running, playing, or otherwise having a great time not coming, it is a different story altogether. Every second your dog does not come, its alternative activities are potently reinforcing its disobedience.

## Active Disobedience

Dogs run off and/or refuse to come when called because they have discovered play and training are mutually exclusive. Consequently, the dog feels the need to run away to have fun. The dog is afraid to go back to its owner because it knows the good times will end. And some dogs are afraid to return to the owner for fear of punishment.

For a dog to blatantly ignore the owner's request to come and to flagrantly continue having a good time is a major training emergency. You must do something drastic, and quickly! Every second you dither around and allow your dog to continue amusing itself strongly rewards the dog for not coming. Basically, your lack of action passively trains your dog to be disobedient! The first item on the agenda is to catch your dog. All the time your dog is running at large, its life is at risk. Once your dog is safely on leash, do not even consider letting it off-leash again until you have trained your dog to come when called, no matter what it is doing or what the distraction.

# 1. First Catch the Dog

A distracted, fleeing dog is much easier to catch than most people think since the dog is usually running towards a distraction. Just walk up to your dog, put it on leash and give it a treat. If, however, your dog is running from you, shouting and running after the dog usually makes it harder to catch. Instead, it is better to run away from the dog, maniacally laughing and shouting the dog's name and then, to drop down on the ground, jerking all fours in the air whilst emitting a high-pitched screech. Most dogs come running pronto. Maybe you will not feel inclined to practice this routine in the park in the course of everyday training, but do remember it for an emergency. It works. And it has already saved the life of several dogs.

Alternatively, you will have to physically and mentally chase the dog down. Unless you have practiced for emergencies, generally it is a bad idea to shout "Come Here." If your dog did not come when called in a normal tone of voice, it is unlikely to come if it thinks you are angry. It is much better to shout an emergency, inhibitory command, such as "Sit!" or "Down!" As a rule during regular training, never switch commands on a dog. Once the dog has been instructed to do something, it must do it. The only exception would be switching to an easier, emergency command in times of stress, confusion, or distraction, as in the above example to change from "Come Here" to "Sit."

Shout "SIT! SIT! SIT!" and continue to do so until your dog sits, and then say, "Good Sit-Stay, Rover." DO NOT GIVE UP! You cannot give up. You have got to catch your dog. If your dog does not sit, but it looks as though it might, lighten-up on the tone and volume, and repeat the command to "Sssssit!," more softly, yet with an emphatic tone. Once your dog sits, tell it to sit-stay, and praise it for a while before you try approaching the dog. Continue to praise the dog in a normal happy voice while you approach to take it by the collar and offer a treat. Approach your dog slowly, and do not get angry, otherwise the dog may bolt again. If you decide to call your dog to you, call it eagerly and happily, running away from your dog as you do so.

No matter how long you have been chasing the dog and no matter what the dog has done when running at large, praise the dog as soon as it starts to come back to you. In fact, praise it every step of the way. When you have the dog on leash, praise it, pet it and maybe give a treat. No matter how difficult this is to do, do it! If you want the dog to eventually come reliably, quickly and eagerly, you had better reward the dog on those unreliable occasions it comes eventually, slowly and dejectedly. There is no point in getting angry at the dog; it was you, who made the mistake of letting an untrained dog off-leash.

NEVER NEVER NEVER punish your dog when it comes back to you. If you do, your dog will take longer to come back the next time, when you, silly owner, let your untrained dog off-leash yet again. Even if your dog has created mayhem in the park when it ran off, if you punish it when it comes back, you will still have a dog which creates mayhem, but now it takes even longer to get under control. If you want to punish your dog, obviously punish it when it is in the act of creating mayhem, but then reward it as it comes back. If you are annoyed, angry, furious or beside yourself with rage, for the meantime, hide your emotions. When the dog is safely back at home, go and bite a pillow, beat a breeze-block or otherwise punish yourself. By all means, let off steam, but do not abuse the dog in the process. Do not punish the dog for your mistakes - you, yes you, let the dog off-leash, left the front door open or kept the dog in a yard knowing full-well it was not escape-proof. Please be happy your dog is still alive. Take a break, and then get back to some sensible training.

## 2. Then Train the Dog

Many owners throw up their hands in despair when their dog runs amuck in the park and fails to come when called. Certainly, training any dog to be reliable in an off-leash and distracting setting can be a daunting prospect which requires a substantial commitment on behalf of the owner. In reality, though, many park-problem dogs are also downright disobedient in a variety of other simpler and safer settings. Few dogs come when called in a safe, fenced dog park. Few will come in dog training class, and some will not even come in from their own backyard. And some dogs will not even sit reliably (as in 100% of the time) when on leash. The point is there is so much training that can be done in safe areas to build a firm foundation of basic control to ready your dog for mastering off-leash, distance, Olympic obedience. Please make sure your dog is reliable at home, in class and on-leash before even thinking of allowing it to run willy-nilly and get itself into trouble in a public place.

There are plenty of safe (fenced) areas to train dogs while they are playing off-leash. The most obvious example would be a dog training class. Or, for example, form a doggy play/training group, and practice in a different owner's backyard each week. Also, it is worth bearing in mind that your dog may be satisfactorily exercised and trained on a long (50-100 feet) line. It is smart to keep your dog on leash and out of trouble. However, it would still be wise to prepare for future potential emergencies and proof the dog to "Sit" or "Come" when you shout. Otherwise, if you shout at your dog when it is running away, it will probably run faster. Heaven forbid, this happens when your dog is running towards a group of children or a busy street. We want the dog to have the confidence to understand that a shouted command conveys urgency and not anger. Even though you may have no intention of letting your dog off-leash again, another person might let the dog escape. Practice training the dog to sit reliably in safe and controlled, yet much more distracting situations, e.g., when playing with other dogs in a fenced yard.

Many dog owners casually let rambunctious dogs off-leash to play and then leash the dog after it comes when called. Now, if an off-leash romp is the reward de rigeur in suburban dogdom, then ending said walk must represent the biggest disappointment or punishment, i.e., unruly behavior is reinforced, and obedient responses are inhibited. This is back to front. At the very least, instruct your dog to sit-stay before letting it off-leash. And if the dog wants to play, obviously the best reward for coming when called is to let your dog go play again. The answer to most recall problems is to repeat "Come Here - Sit - Go Play" over and over throughout the entire play session.

# PLAY RECALLS

To reliably come when called, your dog must learn that play and training need not be mutually exclusive, i.e., coming when called is neither the end of the world nor necessarily the end of the play session. By integrating recalls into play sessions, your dog will learn that if it comes immediately, you will say "Go Play" immediately, whereas if it does not come immediately, the play session is temporarily terminated until the dog eventually comes, i.e., the dog has to come anyway. Basically, we have put Rover's destiny in Rover's paws; Rover can end play by being disobedient, and once the play session has been terminated, only Rover can restart it by obediently going to his owner. By giving the problem (playing with other dogs) a name ("Go Play"), the problem behavior becomes a reward for coming when called. Every time the owner interrupts the play session and requests the dog to come, the owner may then say "Go Play" and thus reward the dog for coming. To keep the play session going, all the dog has to do is to continue to come when called.

Work in a safe area - indoors, in a fenced yard, tennis court, training class or dog park. Initially, work with your dog and just one other - his favorite doggy friend. Whisper-request the dog to come - "Rover, Come Here." If your dog comes, take hold of its collar, praise, pet, pat, hug and treat the critter before saying "Go Play", i.e., just a short, enjoyable time-out from play. If your dog does not come, command it to come - an instructive reprimand - "ROVER!!! Come! Here!" Do not progressively escalate volume and tone over several commands (this would systematically desensitize the dog to your voice). Go from the whisper-request to the all-out, attention-getting command within one second. We want the dog to learn what comes out of our mouths is meaningful, not meaningless.

If your dog comes in response to your reprimand, praise the dog, touch its collar, waggle a food treat in front of its nose but do not give it to the dog. It would be silly to reward your dog after you had to call him twice. Instead, bait the dog with the food, invitingly whisper-request "Come Here," back up two steps, take the dog's collar, give it the treat and say "Go Play," i.e., in order to get a treat and be told "Go

Play," your dog has to come immediately following a single request. If you have to tell the dog twice, repeat the recall until the dog gets it right. The hardest part is getting the dog's attention when it is playing. Once the dog comes, you now have its attention, and it will likely follow the next instruction.

If your dog does not start towards you within one second following your reprimand, the other owner immediately takes hold of Rover's playmate to curtail the play session. Once Rover's playmate has been successfully corralled, it is now your job to get Rover to come. It does not matter how long it takes, Rover will come eventually, if only because there's not much else to do. Once your dog does come, repeat the recall (as described above) until Rover comes on the first request, and then, tell it "Go Play" at which point the other

*Phoenix and Oso waiting*
*to be invited into the living room*

owner instantly releases Rover's playmate, and the play session resumes once more.

Getting your dog to come the first time is the hardest. But, as with all troubleshooting procedures, it gets easier with each attempt. In fact, have the other owner time how long it takes for you to get your dog to come, and you will soon have proof of dramatic improvement within just a few trials. Alternate "Come Here" and "Go Play" over and over, until your dog reliably comes instantaneously in the presence of its favorite playmate. Then, work with another playmate, and then, work with all three together. Eventually, your dog will respond reliably within a large play group.

## LIFE REWARDS

When dealing with behavior problems, we acknowledge the dog is a dog and understandably has a strong need to act like a dog; therefore, we strive to cater to the dog's needs. To apply the same instinctive drive theory to obedience training, it would be true to say that the dog has no need to follow its owner's instructions. Many dogs simply fail to see the point of complying with an endless barrage of repetitive and seemingly irrelevant obedience commands.

First the trainer says "Sit-stay" and then "Come" and then "Sit-stay" and then "Come." "I mean make up your mind. What do you want me to do? - Come or Stay?" The owner says "Heel" and then "Sit," then "Heel" and then "Sit" and so on, and three right turns later, both dog and owner end up where they just started from. The dog must think the owner is silly, or lost. "What's the point? What's the hurry?" The overdrilled dog quickly becomes bored. Its responses lack lustre as it becomes increasingly lethargic, sloppy and unreliable. The level of reprimands increases until the dog actively does not want to comply. And eventually it doesn't.

Conventional rewards, such as praise and food treats, are sufficient during initial instruction and practice, but they are seldom 100% effective when training the dog around distractions. Life rewards are essential to produce a truly reliable dog. As a rule of thumb, the best possible rewards for any dog are the worst distractions in training, i.e., what the dog really wants to do at that

particular moment. Give any problem a name, and train the dog to perform the behavior on cue. Then the owner can bargain "If you do what I want, I'll let you do what you want" i.e., the distraction, which previously was an alternative to good behavior and worked against training, may now be used as a reward to reinforce good behavior, thus working for training.

In the same manner that walking and sniffing were used as rewards for good heeling and playing with other dogs was used as a reward for coming when called, training may be integrated into all the dog's enjoyable activities. For example, although not a natural retriever, Phoenix gladly carries her leash to the front door in expectation of a walk. Remember, your dog's leash is a wonderful lure and reward indoors.

## How To Turn The Dog ON

Choose an emergency, inhibitory control command, such as "Sit" or "Down," and train your dog to respond no matter what it is doing. When dogs are distracted, the hardest command is the first one you give, so make this the simplest, i.e., "Sit." Once your dog sits and you have its attention, the likelihood is greater it will follow additional instructions, such as other inhibitory control commands, e.g., "Down" or maybe more complicated active commands, e.g., "Come Here." However, once your dog is sitting, you have already proved your dog is attentive, compliant and under control, and so most of the times your dog sits obediently, release it immediately.

Make a list of your dog's 20 most enjoyable activities in order of their value, and tape the list on the fridge as a reminder. From now on, every enjoyable activity will have a short training prelude, and every lengthy enjoyable activity will include a host of short training interludes. All we are doing is asking the dog to say, "Please may I do such and such" or "Please may I continue doing such and such" - just basic canine courtesy. "Please" can be anything you want it to be. It can be as short and as simple as an emergency "Sit," as long as a five-minute "Down-Stay," or as involved as a "Sit, Down, Sit-Stay, Stand, Down, Stand-Stay, Down-Stay, Sit-Stay, Come, Heel, Sit, Heel and Sit" sequence.

## Training Preludes

Ask your dog to sit before letting it off-leash, before dinner time, before treats, before coming into the living room, before getting onto the couch, before going outdoors, before coming inside, before you throw its tennis ball etc., and very soon your dog will sit at the drop of a hat.

*Sit means, "Please would you be so kind as to open the car door?"*

## Training Interludes

Periodically, ask your dog to "Sit" several times during on-leash walks, during off-leash walks, during dinner time, when lying on the couch, during play sessions with the owner, during play sessions with other dogs and during games of "Fetch." And before you know it, your dog has joined your team, and the two of you are working together, instead of against each other. Your dog will now see the relevance of what you ask, and so, it will seldom be necessary to enforce your wishes.

By integrating many short (3-5 second) training sessions within all enjoyable activities, eventually your dog will not be able to tell the difference between training and having a good time. Play sessions have become more controlled, and training has become fun. In fact, you have now achieved the highest level in motivational training - natural motivation, i.e., the training exercises themselves have become self-reinforcing. Rewards are no longer necessary during training, because for the dog 'just doing it' has become the reward.

*Moose enjoys
a training interlude
in Central Park*

146

# TRICKS

Tricks are an enjoyable and gratifying aspect of training. How often do we see some old geezer grinning like the proverbial Cheshire cheese, just because his dog shakes hands. Yet, some people think tricks are silly. Others think they are demeaning, and still others think it is cruel to make a dog perform. The mind boggles! Certainly, these people cannot have much fun with their dogs, and neither, for that matter, can their dogs possibly have much fun with them. Killjoys! "Beware of heartless them - given a scalpel they would

*Sandi Thompson and Callahan
1st Place Winners of the KPIX Late Show
Stupid Pet Tricks competition*

dissect a kiss!" To even think teaching animals is inhumane, these people must be using some pretty warped and cruel training techniques. I think these people are wrong. So very wrong. Where on earth is the harm in having fun teaching and communicating with a dog? On the contrary, not training a dog would be inhumane. It would be so cruel not to bother to at least try to open communication channels and teach the dog a few words from our language. Otherwise, the poor dog - our best friend - a social animal - will be subjected to a dumb, mute, asocial existence of never knowing what we would like it to do and therefore, always getting it wrong. The poor dog would be forced to make mistake after mistake and to break rules it never knew existed. That's hardly fair. Let's welcome the dog to our world. Let's teach it our language. And let's talk to our dogs.

Tricks are both enjoyable and extremely useful. Really, dog tricks are not much different from a person performing gymnastics, doing algebra, dancing, sinking a putt or playing the piano - all learned physical and mental skills, practiced to perfection. Similarly, dog tricks are no different from basic obedience commands. Although a lot of dogs perform obedience exercises more reliably than tricks, and a lot of dogs have more fun performing tricks than obedience commands, it need not and, indeed, shouldn't be that way. Tricks should be as precise and reliable as obedience commands - as precise as scoring a perfect 10. And basic obedience should be as much fun as performing tricks - as much fun as dancing.

How often do we see dogs fail to "Sing" or "Speak" on late-night television Stoopid Pet Tricks? How often do we see dogs require six requests before they deign to rollover and play dead? Sloppy! - No reliability, no proofing. Whether a trick or as basic manners, the dog should be trained to do it on the first request. If an American Football quarterback required six requests from the coach to execute the right play, he would soon be sent to the dog house and so should the owner if the dog doesn't "Speak" following a single command.

The good thing about tricks is that everybody smiles, laughs and giggles - the best reward of all. In fact, in no time at all, performing the trick becomes the reward in itself, i.e., the trick becomes self-reinforcing. And the trick becomes a reward for other exercises. Asking the dog to "Give us a hug" is a great reward for a good down-

*A dog must have a pretty solid sit-stay*
*to balance a biscuit bone on its nose*

stay on greetings, and allowing the dog to jump through our arms becomes a rewarding finale for a lightning recall. But how many times do we see highly trained dogs performing ultra-precise heels, recalls, sits and stays - machine perfect but without sparkle - working with owners who give 'praise' that could freeze a frog in Florida? Hey! No one died! Wake up you Scrooges! This is life! Enjoy it! No warm-up laps, no reruns. Have fun with your dog. Now!

Even so, apart from training tricks for fun or to audition for Hollywood, I am still partial towards tricks which have useful applications and tricks that build on basic obedience skills. For example, a dog which balances food on its nose or paws must have a pretty solid stay. Similarly, a dog which retrieves usually has a good recall. A dog which rolls over and plays dead is much easier to groom and flea powder and much more tractable when examined by the veterinarian. A dog which speaks on command may be more easily found when lost or hurt. A dog which backs up may be instructed to give children space while they eat or enable you to open the front door to go out for a walk. Even so, I still grin like a fool when Phoenix shakes hands, sings, rolls over and plays dead. There are so many tricks to teach. Consequently, I have selected just a few of my favorites.

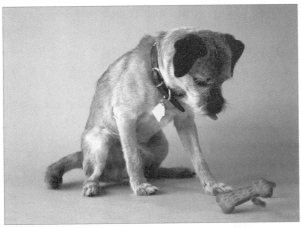

*Whoops!*

## Rollover

Have your pup sit and lie down, and then, keeping the food lure extremely close to the pup's body, instruct the pup to "Rollover," and move the lure backwards along one side of its muzzle to the top of its neck and over its shoulders. It may help if you tickle the doggie's 'doodads' with the other hand. (Physical contact in the inguinal region causes most dogs to raise a hind leg.) As your pup rolls over onto its side and back, keep moving the food lure so that it rolls completely over into the down position once more. Once your puppy has mastered roll-over, a variation is to have the pup roll in the opposite direction with the obvious request, "Now, roll the other way."

## Bang

Another variation of rollover is to have the pup stay on its side or back and play possum. Firstly, try this from the down position. Say "Bang," point your finger like a pistol, move the lure as above, but as soon as the pup is on its side or back, say "Stay" and keep the treat stationary. Secondly, try this from the sitting position. After saying "Bang," give a down signal followed by the rollover signal. Thirdly, try "Bang" from a stand-stay using the combined down- and rollover-signals as before. Finally, try it when the pup is walking. Kids just love this one. So do many adults. "Bang" is the essence of the Omega Rollover.

## Beg

Have your pup sit-stay, say "Beg" and raise the lure a head's length above the puppy's nose, so that it lifts its front paws of the ground and sits back on its haunches. If the pup jumps up, lower the lure and move it backwards a tad. Initially, it may be easier practicing this exercise in a corner, so the puppy may lean against the walls to keep balance.

## Back-up

With your puppy in heel position, sandwiched between yourself and a wall, instruct it to "Back-up," and then move the food lure under the pup's chin and into its brisket. Alternatively, this exercise may be taught in a narrow passageway, such as between a bed and a wall. It is good to alternate "Back-up" with both "Forwards" and "Stand-stay." The concept of forwards and backwards is a good one to learn in other body positions, such as the sit-stay. "Sit Forwards" and "Sit Back" are fine-adjustments to ensure that the dog is ideally placed to set off heeling for example. "Sit Back" is also good when the dog is too eager to get out of the front door.

## Grovel

Start with the pup in a down-stay, and inch the food lure along the ground a little way in front of its nose. If the pup stands up, just try again. Alternatively, move the food lure under some low-slung barrier, such as a bed, coffee table or even under your leg. "Grovel" is helpful for dogs with creeping down-stays. By alternating "Grovel and "Down-Stay," the dog at long-last grasps the essential difference. Now of course, "Grovel," previously the problem that distracted from obedient stays, has become the reward for good down-stays.

## Give Us A Hug

Start with your dog in a sit-stay. Say "Give us a hug," energize the dog by waggling a food lure in front of its nose, and then, slap your chest like a gorilla. It is wise to alternate "Give us a hug" with both sit-stays and down-stays. Thus, the dog learns the difference between enthusiastic and controlled greetings. This wonderful trick is a simple solution for puppies which like to jump-up. First, we train the puppy to sit when greeting people, and then, we may teach the adult dog to jump-up, but only on our terms, i.e., only on cue, when the time is convenient, and we are prepared to enjoy the dog's advances. For example, probably only certain doggy-people will invite the dog to jump up, when they are wearing dog-proof clothing. (The dog-disinterested may be instructed to say "Steady," "Off," "Back-up," "Go to your mat" and "Sit.") On returning home, instruct your dog to down-stay. Formally greet the dog, and then change into dog greeting clothes, and once prepared, ask the dog to jump-up and hug. Now, jumping-up (something the dog likes to do) becomes a reward for a good stay-greeting. Training a dog to shake hands on request is a similar ploy to combat an annoying pawing habit.

## Bow

Instruct your pup to stand, and move the food lure down to the ground to come to rest a few inches in front of the pup's front paws. The puppy will lower its forequarters until elbows and sternum touch the ground. With some pups it is necessary to place the other hand underneath (but without touching) the pup's belly to prevent the hindquarters from collapsing into a down. The playbow posture is a solicitation to play - an 'atmosphere cue' which communicates that subsequent behaviors are playful. This is a wonderful trick for children. If a child can successfully entice the dog to bow, the dog is saying it likes the kid and would like to play, and as such, it is unlikely the dog would be frightened or irritated by the child's antics. Also, "Playbow" is a wonderful instruction to give to your dog when it meets other dogs.

## Turn Around

Have your puppy stand-stay facing you and move the lure in a horizontal circle over the pup's head, so the dog turns in a full circle to come and face you once more. Once your pup learns to turn around, you can teach it to "Turn - The Other Way."

## Dance

Instruct your pup to sit and beg, and then raise the lure a couple of head-lengths, so the puppy stands on its hind legs. Once the pup can balance for several seconds, it may be enticed to walk forwards or to circle as above.

# Fetch

Retrieval is an excellent way to teach vocabulary. Your dog may be instructed to retrieve many different articles, for example, tennis balls and golf balls (make that dog earn its keep), newspapers, neighbor's newspapers, slippers, etc. In so doing, the dog learns the name of each item. Discriminated retrieves have many useful applications in the home. For example, stand by your dog's toy box, and have the dog tidy up the house by retrieving every dog-toy in sight and depositing them in its toy box. Also, dogs are great at finding lost keys, lost baseballs and lost dogs.

Firstly, teach your dog to retrieve exciting objects, such as a tennis ball, chewtoy, bone, or slipper using the "Off"-"Take it"-Thank you" triad. Then, work with less exciting articles. Once the dog reliably retrieves each article by itself, instruct your dog to retrieve one of two articles, then one of three and so on. Give the dog the sun, moon and stars each time it successfully brings back the requested item first try. If it touches, picks up, or brings back the wrong item, just keep repeating the original request until it gets it right, whereupon reward the dog, but this time only moderately. The dog soon learns that incredible rewards are available for retrieving the correct object first try, lesser rewards for eventually getting it right and zip for getting it wrong. Use life rewards. For example, if the dog correctly chooses

*My Dad's dog Dart - lure-reward trained to fetch slippers and find tobacco pouches. Personally, I think Dart used to hide these items just to get attention. Dart also had a breed-specific gundog sense of humour and would charge through the countryside crying out to birds and bunnies "Run! Run! Here comes a man with a gun!"*

155

to bring its leash, it gets to go on a walk, or if it correctly retrieves its tennis ball, you will throw it.

NEVER punish the dog for making the wrong choice. Not only will punishment deter the dog from making further wrong choices, but also it will deter the dog from making any choice at all, i.e., the dog will stop retrieving. If you become frustrated with your dog's poor performance (i.e., your poor teaching), retrieve the articles yourself, sit down, calm down... and try again tomorrow.

## Go to... Commands

The "Go to..." commands are another wonderful vocabulary learning tool. The puppy may be trained to go to places, for example, its mat, bed, basket, or crate, to go outside, inside, upstairs or downstairs, to get in the back seat of the car or front seat, to get off the couch and on the couch, etc., or to go to different people. In teaching these exercises, the puppy learns the names of different locations in the home and the names of different family members and friends.

## Go to Places

Request your pup to "Go to your mat," show the puppy a food lure, run and put it on the pup's mat. As soon as the pup reaches its mat, it may pick up the food lure as a reward. At a later stage in training, put the reward on the pup's mat before telling it to go there. The puppy learns it is highly beneficial to follow the owner's advice and check out its mat when told, even if the owner has nothing of value on their person. When the pup reaches its mat, ask it to settle down. Periodically, give the pup treats whilst it remains on its mat. Dogs may be trained to go to a variety of locations using this method.

A quicker way to train inside/outside, upstairs/downstairs, on/off the couch and back seat/front seat locations is to take a bunch of dry kibble from the puppy's dinner bowl, and for example, stand on the threshold of the back door and to randomly alternate the requests "Outside" and "Inside." After saying "Outside," throw a piece of kibble outside, and after saying "Inside," throw a piece of kibble indoors. The pup soon learns to predict the direction of jettisoned kibble from the owner's instruction and quickly scampers in the appropriate direction.

*Your dog will become quite a seasoned performer with a combination of "Go to..." and "Touch..." commands*

Place commands are wonderful, particularly in times of stress or confusion, e.g., when a gaggle of infant and adult monsters crowd the front door at Hallowe'en, whenever the dog is in the way or just acting like a plain jerk. With a single command - "Go to your mat," "Downstairs," or "Outside," the dog is under control once more.

## Go to People

When two people are training the pup at the same time, it is possible to do yo-yo recalls back and forth. Dad asks the pup to sit and then instructs it (once only) "Rover, Go to Mother." Mother waits one second and then calls Rover. After doing a little obedience and/or trick routine with the pup, Mother tells it, "Rover, Go to Dad." Dad waits one second and then, calls the pup and so forth. The puppy quickly learns when one person says "Go to..." the other person calls and gives me a treat. Since the pup is eager to help the owner's training, it rushes to the other person as soon as the "Go to...," request is given, i.e., the pup has anticipated the recall and learned the meaning of the "Go to..." request. This time it receives several treats and a hug.

Working with just two people, the puppy may anticipate recalls at inappropriate times and run back and forth between the two owners without any instruction being given. A profitable way around this problem is to practice round-robin recalls with three or more people. As before, one person instructs the pup "Go to Jamie," and Jamie calls the pup after one second. The puppy cannot just dart off to the other person to get a reward, since there are two or more people to choose from. Instead, the pup has to wait for the full instruction to identify the name of the person. If it goes to the right person, it gets wonderfully rewarded, but if it goes to the wrong person, it is ignored.

"Go to people" commands may be practiced with different people spread out in different rooms of the house or on walks outdoors. It is one of the quickest ways to exercise a dog to exhaustion with minimal expenditure of energy on behalf of the owners. On walks, owners may instruct their German Wirehair, for example, to run back and forth and cover nearly 20 miles while the owners walk barely a mile.

"Go to people" commands have many uses with the family, which now has its very own Search and Rescue dog. If little Johnny is lost on a camping trip, Dad can instruct Rover to "Go to Jamie," and good old Rove can use his vastly superior olfactory powers to track down the little worm. Alternatively, tie a note to Rover's collar, and our faithful friend may be used to deliver messages to another person, such as "Time to come inside for dinner," "Pleeeease bring some coffee upstairs" or "Come up to the television room and change the channel." Hey, now we're talking!

*Team SIRIUS DIRT collects First Place ribbons after setting a*
*World Record in the Woof Relay (sponsored by Big Dog Sportswear)*
*at the 1996 PuppyDog AllStars K9-GAMES in Long Beach, California*

# HOW TO TEACH A NEW DOG OLD TRICKS

# IV. TRAINING THEORY
## Why Does it Work?

When the great American psychologist Edward Lee Thorndike embarked upon his series of animal learning studies on operant conditioning and behavior modification, he first sought the help of dog trainers to discover how animals learned. Now, over one hundred years later, the tide has turned, and dog trainers are beginning to look to the field of animal learning to discover more efficient and effective training methods. Most trainers are at least aware of the names Pavlov and Skinner and of the terms classical conditioning and behavior modification, but few are aware of the abundance of available information in the annals of the psychological sciences. Research findings are published in an academic jargon, which is confusing and/or virtually unintelligible for people who might otherwise put the material to excellent practical use. Consequently, even to this day, research is seldom applied in animal training.

The arbitrary division of learning research into separate areas of classical and operant conditioning is the product of laboratory study. Many psychologists, especially those with a strictly academic bent, tend to place an unrepresentative emphasis on minor theoretical differences between these two types of conditioning, fostering a further divergence between the two fields. A schismatic approach is theoretically unfounded and extremely counterproductive for the useful practical application of research findings.

In reality, classical and operant conditioning are merely theoretical analyzes of different aspects of the same basic learning sequence. Basically, the study of operant conditioning mainly concerns the modification of the incidence of behaviors, whereas the study of classical conditioning addresses the acquisition of stimulus control of behavior or putting behaviors on cue. From a practical viewpoint, it makes sense to combine the best of both scientific approaches and apply them to the art of training dogs, other animals and people. Thus, the basic training sequence comprises:

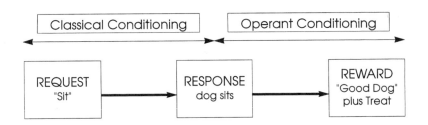

## Increasing the Incidence of Behaviors

*Thorndike's First Law of Effect* states that the frequency of a behavior is dependent upon its immediate outcome. If the outcome is pleasant, the behavior will increase in frequency. For example, if Larry Labrador jumps on its owner, who is returning from the supermarket with a bag of groceries, and the dog steals a string of sausages, Larry will be more likely to jump-up to greet its owner in the future. Thus, in the basic training sequence, rewarding the dog reinforces its preceding response, which therefore increases in frequency.

## Stimulus Control

The purpose of training a dog is not simply to train the dog how to sit, for example. A four-week-old puppy knows how to sit! Neither is training limited to altering the frequency of existing behaviors. The owner does not just want a dog which spends more time sitting. Instead, the owner wants a dog which sits reliably when requested. Thus, from a functional viewpoint, the major purpose of dog training is for the owner to establish stimulus control over the dog's behavior, so the dog will perform on cue.

In the basic training sequence, not only does the reward a)

reinforce the preceding response, which therefore b) increases in frequency, but also the reward c) reinforces or strengthens the association between the request and the appropriate response, thus d) increasing the likelihood that the dog will perform the response on cue, i.e., following the trainer's request. Eventually, the dog will learn that it is only rewarded if it sits when told to do so. This is the essence of training.

## Enticing The Dog To Respond Correctly

The science of dog training consists of only a couple of dozen or so rules and theoretical principles similar to those described above. Most of these can be mastered in a short study course. The art of dog training, however, is a little more complex, and the trainer's skill progressively improves with continued practice and experience. For the most part, the success of training depends upon the trainer's knack of successfully predicting when an animal will behave appropriately, so it may be requested to do so beforehand and rewarded for doing so immediately afterwards. Rather than waiting for the dog to perform spontaneously, mastery in training is reflected by the trainer's ability to entice or to lure, the dog to perform the desired behavior, so that training proceeds quickly, smoothly and effortlessly. After requesting the dog to "Sit" for example, the trainer uses a lure to entice it to sit. Once the dog sits, it may be given the lure as a reward or rewarded in some other fashion. Thus, in lure/reward training, the basic training sequence comprises:

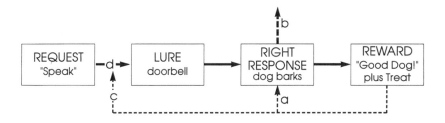

Using lure/reward training methods, it is possible to teach a vast repertoire of responses without ever touching, guiding or forcing the dog. Not touching the dog during initial training is of paramount importance. In the absence of physical prompts, the dog learns to pay selective attention to verbal instructions and hand (lure) movements from the outset. Thus, the dog more quickly learns the meaning of verbal commands and hand signals, which form the very foundation for distance control and instructive reprimands.

By all means touch (pet and pat) your dog as a reward for responding correctly. However, if your dog is physically prompted or guided into position, i.e., it is touched before it sits, the dog will selectively attend to the physical contact rather than the verbal command. With the exception of a few important Larsonian words, such as 'walkies' and 'dindins', most of what we say is irrelevant to dogs. But touching the dog is always relevant. The dog has learned that touch means petting or punishment. When touching and talking to your dog at the same time, the dog will respond preferentially to the physical cue, because it is more important. It is as if your dog never even hears the instruction, since physical contact tends to overshadow or mask verbal chatter. Certainly, your dog may quickly learn to sit when you touch or pull on its collar and/or touch or push on its rump, but it will take much longer for your dog to learn the meaning of the word 'sit', because training has now become a two-step process. You have only taught your dog to respond to physical prompting; you still have to teach your dog to respond to verbal instructions in order to establish distance control off-leash.

If training is limited to leash work, physical prompts and punishments, you will experience control problems when your dog is at a distance and at other times when you cannot touch it. Your dog may be quite well behaved on-leash, but off-leash obedience is much less reliable, if evident at all. Moreover, the transition from on-leash to off-leash training is extremely slow and laborious. In contradistinction, it is easier, quicker, more effective, more efficient, more enjoyable and much safer to simply lure/reward train your dog off-leash and establish verbal and distance control from the outset. Once lure/reward trained off-leash, you may put your dog on-leash to take it for a walk. This will not reduce your control over your dog at all, rather it will enhance it.

# Decreasing the Incidence of Behaviors

*Thorndike's Law of Effect* also states that if the outcome of a behavior is unpleasant, the behavior will decrease in frequency. For example, if our Labrador friend jumps on its returning owner, who accidentally drops a couple of dozen cans of dog food on the dog's head, then Larry would be less likely to jump on the owner in the future.

## Binomial Feedback

When attempting to communicate with organisms which do not understand our language, whether they be animals, pre-verbal children, foreigners or non-verbal husbands, all information must be converted to a binomial interface which is understood by both parties. Thus, the trainer's feedback, which reflects and modifies the dog's behavior, must be either positive or negative - a series of 'yesses' and 'noes' - rewards and reprimands. There are four types of binomial feedback, two of which are essential in training and two of which are not:

1. Reward vs. No Reward
2. Reward vs. Reprimand
3. No Reward vs. No Reprimand
4. Reprimand vs. No Reprimand

## 1. Reward vs. No Reward

Reward vs. No Reward is the nature of the binomial feedback when teaching your dog firstly, the meaning of your instructions and secondly, the relevance of your instructions, i.e., teaching the dog what to do and why it should do it. This would be true whether teaching a young puppy or when teaching an older dog new tricks.

Your dog will learn: if I get it right, I get rewarded; whereas if I don't, I don't. During initial training, receiving no praise, pats or treats is sufficient 'punishment' for making mistakes. Although, at this stage we can hardly call them mistakes. Your dog cannot possibly know what is wrong if you have yet to complete teaching it what is right. Nonetheless, in a relatively short time, your dog will quickly appreciate that it is in its best interests to follow your instructions. And soon, your dog will want to comply.

Receiving no rewards for not getting it right is much more of a disappointment to your dog during relevancy training, because the rewards are now much more valuable and meaningful, i.e., life rewards. Not surprisingly, your dog will learn extremely quickly that it is in its very best interests to follow your instructions, and consequently, your dog will really want to comply.

When reliability really matters, for example when training search and rescue and bomb-detection dogs, a Reward vs. No Reward feedback is the cutting-edge technique. Many dogs may be quickly trained to a whopping 95% reliability level without employing a single punishment!

## 2. Reward vs. Reprimand

Once you are absolutely certain your dog understands both the meaning and relevance of your instructions, it is time to proof your dog's performance and enforce correct responses at all times. If your dog gets it right, it is handsomely rewarded, but if it gets it wrong, it is reprimanded, and it still has to do it correctly anyway. But hold your horses! Before you rush ahead and get on your dog's case, let's define a few terms here. How do you know your dog understands the meaning of your instructions? And what do you understand by the terms 'enforce' and 'reprimand'?

The first item on your agenda is to test your dog's comprehension. Take your dog out into the backyard, and let it wander around. For the next five minutes, every time the second hand on your watch passes 20, 35, 40 and 60 seconds, quietly instruct your dog to sit. That comprises a total of 20 requests in five minutes. If your dog sits 19 out of 20 times, it is working at a 95% reliability level, and it has a very good understanding of your verbal instruction to sit (in the yard, without other distractions), and it is well prepared for you to proof its performance (in the yard, without other distractions) by enforcing correct responses. If it sits less than 19 times, it is not ready. So, go back and do some more reward training. Using this simple test you will also find your dog's reliability varies considerably depending on 1) where it is being tested (in the kitchen, yard, or park), 2) the nature of the distractions present (smells, children, other dogs and squirrels) and 3) the identity of the trainer (you, a family member, a friend or a stranger).

I have used the word 'enforce' to mean you 'urge' your dog to comply or you 'compel' it to behave by 'exerting your influence'. 'Enforce' does not mean physically force or even mentally traumatize your dog. 'Enforcing' correct responses simply means that once you ask your dog to sit, it is going to sit and that's that. It is not going to sit because of something nasty, but rather it is going to sit because you are not going to give up on the training session until it does. Basically, 'enforce' means it is now time to be consistent in training by calmly insisting on consistent responses from your dog. Even though your request to sit is given in a pleasant tone, the notion that the dog must comply is now implicit in the instruction, i.e., the 'whisper-request' is now a softly spoken 'command' or a 'warning' to your dog that it will be reprimanded if it does not immediately obey.

By 'reprimanded' of course we mean instructively reprimanded, i.e., not only letting the dog know it is on the wrong track but also, letting it know how to make amends. Reprimand does not mean punish, and it certainly does not entail frightening or hurting the dog.

When enforcing correct responses, the basic training sequence now becomes:

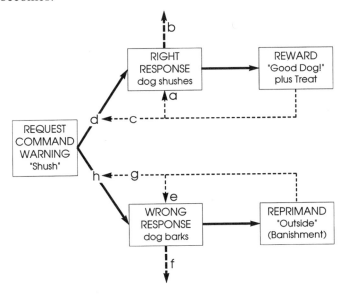

Your request (command/warning) now represents a fork in the road, presenting your dog with a choice of how to behave. If your dog makes the right choice, the reward a) reinforces the right response, which b) increases in frequency. Also, the reward c) strengthens the association between the request and the desired behavior, which d) increases the likelihood that the dog will make this choice in the future. However, if your dog makes the wrong choice, the reprimand e) inhibits the wrong response, which f) decreases in frequency. Also, the reprimand g) strengthens the association between the warning and the undesired behavior, which therefore, h) decreases the likelihood the dog will make the wrong choice on future occasions. Within time, the request will reliably elicit the desired behavior.

## 3. No Reward vs. No Reprimand

At first glance, nothing vs. nothing may appear to be no feedback at all regarding the dog's performance. By providing no feedback, the dog will never learn what the owner considers to be right and wrong. Yet, in a sense, the dog does receive feedback from an owner who provides no feedback. The dog learns that it can do exactly what it likes. Providing no feedback when working with the dog is the most common fault of novice trainers.

All we have to do in training is 1) instruct the dog what is right and reward it for desirable behavior and then 2) show the dog what is wrong and reprimand the dog for undesirable behavior. So simple. Yet the average novice dog owner can do neither. If failing to reward a dog (spouse, child or employee) for desired behavior is the quintessential human foible in any interaction but especially during teaching/training, then failing to instructively reprimand a dog (spouse, child or employee) must come a very close second. For example, the young dog comes when called on numerous occasions, and the owner does not say so much as a thank you. Performing tasks without reward becomes both a bore and a chore, and so, eventually the dog runs off, and for the most part, the owner watches dumb struck. In the absence of feedback from the owner, the dog provides its own feedback. The dog will indulge in those behaviors it finds to be self-reinforcing, i.e., behaviors most likely viewed by the owner as misbehavior.

Some obedience competitions forbid the use of rewards or reprimands. However, 'no reward vs. no reprimand' feedback is not an ingredient of an instructional program. Rather, it represents the end-point of training - the final performance - whereby the dog happily, willingly, reliably and precisely follows the handler's instructions without any feedback whatsoever. Although, of course, it is impossible to teach the dog without feedback, it is important for all dog owners, especially potential obedience competitors, to practice short periods of 'training' with no feedback, in order to prepare the dog for similar real-life situations.

## 4. Reprimand vs. No Reprimand

There is absolutely no productive role for punishment-training in any aspect of teaching or training animals or people. Sadly though, 'ignoring the good and punishing the bad' is a ubiquitous human failing, which contaminates all human interactions, including inter-spousal, parent-child, teacher-pupil, employer-employee and person-pet relationships. There are still some dog trainers who punish a dog even though it understands neither the meaning nor the relevance of their seemingly silly 'instructions'. Certainly, the dog will learn, but it will learn all the wrong things. Firstly, the dog will learn to dislike the entire training experience, notwithstanding the trainer. Secondly, the dog will discover all those occasions when the trainer can not punish the dog for misbehaving. And on those occasions, the dog will have a ball and do exactly what it wants.

## Criteria for Rewards and Punishments

Rewards and punishments must meet a number of absolute criteria. Punishments must be effective but not overbearing, and to be effective, punishments should be instructive, immediate and consistently administered. Above all, the dog must be warned beforehand, so it has adequate opportunity to avoid punishment by acting appropriately as previously trained, i.e., for punishments to be really effective, the dog must know the acceptable alternatives. Similarly, rewards must be effective but not over-exciting, they must be immediate, and for maximal effect, rewards should be quantitatively and qualitatively variable and administered according to a differential reinforcement schedule.

## Reprimands

The first and foremost criterion for punishment is tautological - that punishment is punishing, i.e., it is effective. If not effective, 'punishment' is nothing more than plain old abuse. Repeated punishments for the same crime is the first danger signal punishments are not effective. Punishing the dog is obviously not working, and so, it's time to change to Plan B.

Punishment must be sufficiently strong to produce the desired effect but not so extreme as to destroy the dog's concentration or its confidence and trust in the owner. Owners should beware of using punishment to successfully eliminate a behavior problem, yet severely damaging the dog's temperament and ruining its relationship with the owner in the process. Beware of winning the battle but losing the war. In terms of the degree of severity, the punishment should fit the crime. It is a severe crime for an adult dog to snap and lunge, for example, whereas it is a comparatively minor misdemeanor for a young pup to poop on a Persian rug.

The dog must know precisely why it is being punished. The relevance of punishment depends very much on its immediacy. If the dog's 'crime' is immediately followed by punishment, the dog will get the picture.

Delayed punishments do not work, and they are extremely dangerous. Punishment inhibits the immediately preceding action. Therefore delayed discipline primarily punishes the dog: for greeting its owner, for approaching or returning to its owner and/or for allowing its owner to approach and take hold of the dog. The dog will quickly become hand-shy and leery of the owner's proximity. If the owner wants to punish the dog for owner-absent behaviors, for running off or for breaking a stay, they should do so immediately. If they do not know how to do this, they should seek help from someone who does. Better still, do not give the dog the opportunity to misbehave - keep it confined or on-leash until properly trained. Thus, it will not misbehave, and there will be no need for punishment at all.

Verbal reprimands are far more effective compared with physical punishments. Reprimands may be administered instantaneously and from a distance, whereas it takes time to approach and take hold of the dog to administer a non-specific 'Owie'. Also, instructive reprimands are inherently specific and informative, whereas physical reprimands are neither. "Quickly!," "Steady!," "Sit!," "Off!," "Gently!," "Outside!," "Shush!," "Chewtoy!"are all examples of effective instructive reprimands, in which a single word informs the dog 1) it is about to make a error and 2) how to rectify the mistake. The volume and tone of the trainer's voice reprimand the dog, but the instruction immediately informs the dog how to put things right, so that it may avoid further punishment and instead, be praised for behaving acceptably. For example, when told to "SIT!," the dog knows without a doubt 1) it is doing something wrong and 2) the owner wants it to sit. However, there is usually confusion when, for example, repeated and non-instructive leash corrections are dispensed during a heeling exercise - the dog may not know whether the owner wants it to hurry up, slow down, move away, move closer, sit, sit-straight, smile, break wind or whatever.

As far as possible, the trainer must always endeavor to give the dog an opportunity to avoid any kind of punishment whatsoever by opting to behave appropriately as previously trained. For behaviors the owner considers to be undesirable at all times (e.g., jumping on strangers or chasing children and livestock), the dog must know its alternatives. The owner must first teach the dog acceptable behavior and then instruct the dog accordingly in each situation. For example, to tell the dog to "Sit" when greeting people.

Avoidance training is much more effective than simple punishment training. During proofing, implicit in the request "Sit" is a warning the dog will be reprimanded if it does not sit. Hence, the dog has the opportunity to sit in order to avoid punishment. For behaviors the owner considers to be sometimes acceptable and sometimes not (e.g., barking), the owner should always warn the dog ("Shush!") before punishing it. If the owner does not warn the dog but simply punishes the dog when it misbehaves (punishment training), the dog can neither avoid the punishment (inhumane) nor learn the meaning of the warning (inane).

In order for punishment training, aversive conditioning and avoidance training to be effective, the dog must be punished each and every time it misbehaves. Failure to punish the dog just once will produce problems... BIG problems! Realizing there are some situations when it is not punished, the dog will become a situational misbehaver, e.g., an owner-absent misbehaver.

## Rewards

Rewards must be rewarding. Each dog has its own reward hierarchy, which differs from dog to dog. Each dog will value some rewards over others, and the relative value of different rewards will vary from day to day and from moment to moment. For example, on occasions, previously high-valued rewards may have no reinforcing value and may even be inhibitory or irritating to the dog. There is no point in trying to pet and praise a dog or force fragments of freeze-dried liver between its flews, if all the dog wants to do is romp with other dogs. Praise, petting and food rewards may no longer be rewarding. "Go play" is the only reward that will work effectively at that time, i.e., the owner must convert the distraction, which prompts misbehavior, into a reward to reinforce good behavior.

Rewards must be immediate. Delaying rewards always reinforces the wrong behaviors. For example, if the dog is playing with other dogs and immediately responds with a Mach 3 bullet-recall, do not delay praise because the dog may sit sloppily or jump-up. Delaying rewards also risks the calamitous possibility that desirable behavior may be inhibited. For example, if, following a good recall, the dog is punished for jumping-up, not only does the punishment strongly inhibit jumping-up, but also, it partially inhibits the good recall. Eventually, the dog will not come when called. Instead, immediately rewarding the dog for good behavior and similarly, immediately reprimanding the dog for bad behavior will have the desired effect of reinforcing the good and inhibiting the bad.

There are several thousand published scientific studies on the single question of when, or when not, to reward an animal for correct responses, in order to achieve the quickest learning and best retention. Psychological research has used a number of different reinforcement schedules:

1. Continuous Reinforcement (CR)
2. Fixed Ratio (FR)
3. Fixed Interval (FI)
4. Variable Ratio (VR)
5. Variable interval (VI)
6. Differential (DR)

Continuous reinforcement schedules really only exist in the laboratory, wherein rewards are normally dispensed according to a computer program. CR schedules have little efficacious use in dog training. Firstly, no trainer possesses computer-like capabilities to consistently reward a dog for each and every correct response. Secondly, with continuous reinforcement, following an initial learning spree, the dog's responses eventually become sloppy and unreliable.

Similarly, other 'fixed' reinforcement schedules are constructs of academic research and are notoriously ineffective in the practical arena. Strangely though, fixed schedules are widely used for human training, where they are equally ineffective! For example, with fixed-interval schedules, the subject is rewarded after a fixed time interval. The major problem with 'wage-reinforcement' and 'payday-rewards' is that the employees tend to 'goof-off,' since they know they are going to get paid anyway whether they work or not. Also, the quality of work will vary. Towards the end of the week with Friday payday imminent, all the employees are working up a storm. Not so Monday morning! Similarly with spoiled dogs, it is not uncommon to lose the dog's attention and participation immediately after giving a treat. Fixed-ratio schedules, e.g., piece-rate, wherein the subject is rewarded after a fixed number of responses, cause 'ratio-strain' and problems of 'quality control'. If the number of responses (pieces) required for reward (unit pay) is too large, the subject gives up trying and goes on strike. If the subject works quickly, to perform many responses (produce more pieces), to earn more rewards (more money), the quality of individual responses takes a nose-dive.

Rewarding the dog according to a variable reinforcement schedule, e.g., using variable-ratio and/or variable-interval schedules is much more effective than rewarding the dog after every correct response. Using a variable-ratio schedule, the dog is rewarded for performing an average number of correct responses. For example, by rewarding the dog after three correct changes of body position, then after six changes, then after two and then after nine, the dog has been rewarded on average after every five correct responses (VR5) and actually received four rewards for a total of 20 correct responses. Similarly, using a variable-interval schedule and rewarding the dog, for example, after three seconds of sit-stay, then after 12 seconds, then after five seconds and then after 20, the dog has been rewarded on average after every 10 seconds of sit-stay (VR10) and has received four rewards for 40 seconds of cumulative sit-stay.

For most exercises, a variable schedule may be used from the outset, since using lure/reward techniques, most dogs get it right on the first or second try. Many exercises are all-or-none responses - either the dog gets it right or it doesn't. If it gets it right on the first try, immediately start to stretch the ratio, and ask the dog to perform two responses for a reward or to respond for a little longer on successive tries. If the dog does not get it right on the first try - try again.

Similarly, when shaping procedures are used to teach more complex commands, whereby the dog is rewarded a number of times in a row for performing successive approximations to the desired response, each reinforced response is a little better than the one before, and once the dog has mastered the entire task, the ratio is stretched as before.

It is actually extremely important not to reward the dog every time it performs the same behavior. If the dog is rewarded after each and every correct response, it will learn quickly, but then it will also forget quickly! On the other hand, if the dog is rewarded only occasionally and at random, it will learn almost as quickly, it will remember better and it will strive to do better. The dog will continue responding to the owner's requests for over a much longer time, and it will perform each response with more enthusiasm.

Why should a variable schedule produce better retention and reliability, if the dog is receiving, say, one-tenth of the number of rewards it would get on a continuous reinforcement schedule? There are several explanations. If the dog is rewarded for every correct response, it will receive many rewards, and thus, the rewards progressively lose value and novelty as the dog becomes satiated. Moreover, knowing it will certainly be rewarded when it eventually responds, the dog may wonder, "What's the hurry?" Or the dog may decide it will do it the next time, because it knows the reward will still be there. This is why shops have sales; people rush in before the bargains disappear. Certainty spawns complacency.

Repeated, expected rewards quickly become boring, whereas occasional, unexpected rewards are always lovely surprises. Comparing the schedules of a slot machine (VR) and a coffee-vending machine (CR) is an illuminating exercise. People quickly become slaves to a slot machine. Each dollar is eagerly and enthusiastically dispensed with the 'absolute knowledge' (desperate hope) that this one will win the big one. If they do not win, they try again... and again and again and again! It is not uncommon for players not to win for several tries in a row before eventually being tickled by a teeny reward - 'two cherries'. Two cherries for Heaven's sake! People operate slot machines for hours on end, enjoyably maintained on a pathetically simple VR - repeatedly performing a boring manual operant - all for the elusive jackpot, which, in probability, they will never win. However, people put quarters in coffee machines with bored detachment. If the machine fails to deliver - just once, the person becomes unglued, kicks the machine and storms off in a temper. And would they put another bunch of quarters into a dysfunctional machine? Of course not! Well, neither would a dog.

With a continuous reinforcement schedule, the dog may stop responding the first time it does not get a reward, because it only takes one trial for the dog to learn that the machine is empty, e.g., the owner does not have any food treats, or perhaps, the owner is angry and does not have much affection to share with the dog. The owner's control over the dog becomes reward-dependent. If the owner has rewards to give, the dog may do it, but if the owner has no rewards, the dog will not do it at all. On the other hand, using a variable schedule, the dog is often not rewarded for several trials in succession, so the dog keeps trying with the hope that this recall will win the jackpot - or two cherries, at least.

Rewarding the dog according to a variable schedule - at random for correct responses - will produce and maintain an eager and reliable performer. However, if, for example, we are going to reward the dog on average once for every 10 correct responses, when should we give the rewards? After each initial response - to whet the dog's appetite? After each fifth response - in case the dog is getting bored? Or, after each complete sequence of 10 responses? No. All of these schedules would be simple and ineffective FR10's. At least, reward the dog according to a true VR10, giving five rewards at random over 50 correct responses. But surely, we can do better than a hard-wired, soft-programmed computer, because in addition to making quantitative assessments of the dog's responses, we humans are able to make complex subjective judgments vis a vis the quality of the dog's behavior.

Obviously, it makes sense to reward the dog for its best responses. With a differential reinforcement schedule, the dog is rewarded differentially according to the quality of its behavior. To even be considered for any reward the dog must perform an above-average response. For even better responses, the dog receives even better rewards, and for the very best responses, the dog receives the very best rewards and maybe an occasional jackpot! Moreover, as training proceeds, the owner may progressively refine the criteria that dictate whether or not the dog's performance is worthy of a particular level of reward. Hence, training becomes an ever-learning, ever-improving process of repeatedly shaping, honing and fine-tuning the dog's behavior.

## Rewards or Punishments?

Never has there been a more hotly debated topic in the field of dog training than whether to use reward-oriented or punishment-oriented training methods. Lure/reward methods used to be quite common for training all sorts of domestic animals up until the turn of the century. However, following the two World Wars, force/punishment methods became the sine qua non for training military dogs and by the 50's and 60's, the 'military method' was the accepted way to train all dogs, pet dogs included. With some landmark written works by Leon Whitney (1963), Ed Beckman (1979) and Gail Burnham (1980), the tide began to turn and now lure/reward, play-training methods are very much in vogue once more.

Learning to achieve the correct balance between the use of enticement and enforcement is the secret to successful training. Both rewards and reprimands are essential to produce a truly reliable and enthusiastically obedient dog. Punishments have absolutely no place when teaching the meaning and relevance of our requests, but corrections and instructive reprimands are necessary when enforcing commands. A good working ratio is 10 rewards for each reprimand. Even so, each correction or reprimand is an advertisement the dog does not yet adequately understand the meaning and/or the relevance of our instructions. By all means, reprimand the dog in an emergency, but then 1) repair the damage to the dog/owner relationship and 2) go back to square one and teach the dog properly.

Compared to force/punishment training, lure/reward training methods are easier, more enjoyable, more effective and more efficient - the dog will learn quicker and remember longer.

## Ease

It is difficult and often impossible for some owners to master the many and various techniques for reprimanding, correcting and punishing dogs during training. As such, many methods of punishment are utterly inappropriate for family training. How, for example, can a six-year-old child administer a simple leash correction, let alone an 'alpha-rollover'? The very idea is both preposterous and potentially dangerous. (An alpha-rollover involves grabbing the dog by its cheeks and flipping it onto its back, i.e., for the owner to impersonate the big bad boss of the wolf pack and supposedly to teach the dog who's boss!!! This is not training; this is abuse. And also, it is a surefire way to get people bitten and to get dogs euthanized. Real dumb 'advice'.)

On the other hand, every family member can say "Good doggie" -

even two-year-olds. Well, nearly every family member. Some men have difficulty praising dogs, especially in public, and when they do, the 'praise' sounds like they are commiserating with a moribund sea slug on metaldehyde. Some people may not be able to praise convincingly, but the dog gets the message when it gets the treat. This is a primary reason why we use food in training.

## Enjoyment

It is enjoyable to reward but unpleasant to punish. Training with bountiful rewards is fun for the owner and fun for the dog, whereas a punishment-oriented program is hardly a joyful enterprise for either party. Repeated punishments make training as much as a drag for the dog as it is an unpleasant chore for the owner.

As a wonderful side-effect of obedience training, each reward improves the dog's view of its human companion, cementing the bond between owner and dog. On the other hand, repeated punishments progressively destroy the dog's trust and respect in its owner, as they insidiously undermine the very foundations of the dog/owner relationship.

With the administration of excessive or extreme punishment, there is always the danger that the dog might associate punishment with the owner rather than with the misbehavior. Many dogs are convinced that it cannot be their behavior which is unacceptable, because on many occasions, it misbehaves without punishment. Rather than learning the behavior has unpleasant consequences, the dog learns the presence of the owner has unpleasant consequences. The dog develops a Jekyll and Hyde type personality. It has a great time being a dog and enjoys exquisite 'separation relief' when the owner is absent, out of sight or out of reach, but it suffers a depressing inhibited time when the owner is present.

## Effectiveness

In order for punishment training to be truly effective, the dog must be consistently punished each and every time it misbehaves. This is virtually impossible outside of a laboratory setting. Human beings are not computers, and they are never 100% consistent. Consequently, the dog soon learns that punishment is contingent upon the owner's physical presence and/or mental awareness. Ultimately, the dog discovers situations when its misbehavior goes unpunished, such as when the owner is absent, when the owner is physically present but mentally absent (e.g., daydreaming) or when the owner is physically present but functionally absent (e.g., when the dog is off-leash and beyond the owner's reach and physical corrections are impossible). An over-reliance on punishments in training is the harbinger of 'owner-absent problems' and 'ring-wise dogs'.

On the other hand, it is actually advantageous to be inconsistent when rewarding correct behaviors. This is indeed a fortuitous state of affairs for human trainers. Herein lies the difference between the effectiveness of reward training and punishment training. Using punishment training, let just one misbehavior go unpunished, and you have a big problem. However, using reward training, it is more effective to reward the dog only occasionally and even at random. Furthermore, by refining a variable reinforcement schedule into a differential reinforcement schedule, reward training becomes an extremely powerful teaching tool.

## Efficiency

From a practical viewpoint, whereas there are numerous ways a dog may get it wrong, there is *ONLY ONE RIGHT WAY*. There are many, many ways for the trainee to err. Animals and children especially have an inimitable mastery of a frighteningly comprehensive repertoire of umpteen and sundry mistakes and misbehaviors for any given training exercise. For some dogs, the number of inappropriate improvisations on a given theme is infinite. Using punishment training, it would be necessary to punish the dog each and every time it misbehaves. Thus, by definition, punishment-training is actually impossible, since it would take an infinite amount of time. Indeed, punishment training becomes the Myth of Sisyphus - a never-ending quest to disprove the null hypotheses. On the other hand, it takes considerably less time to teach the dog the single correct response from the outset. If you have in mind how you would like your dog to act, don't keep it a secret from the dog - teach it!

*HOW TO TEACH A NEW DOG OLD TRICKS*

# V. PHYSICAL HEALTH

Your dog's general health and longevity are of paramount importance. All temperament, behavior and training issues pale in the face of sickness and death. Some dogs have frequent injuries or illnesses, whereas others have always been the epitome of good health. Some dogs die at an early age, whereas others are still raring to go at 14 or 15. You are going to spend a lot of time playing, training and just hanging out with your new dog. You are going to get to know your dog as a friend and you're going to treasure its company. You'll miss it when its gone. And so 1) do your best to select a dog which stands a good chance of sticking around for 16 years or so and then, 2) make sure to enjoy and appreciate your dog while it is still alive and kicking.

It is not always possible to check on the longevity and general health of your puppydog's forebears. Sometimes adopting an older dog or picking a puppy can be akin to buying a pig in a poke. However, an investigatory health and longevity check is certainly the number one priority when obtaining a puppy from a breeder.

Be sure to check if your puppy comes from a positively geriatric line of dogs that utterly revel in good health during their sunset years. Ask to see your potential puppy's relations, especially its parents, grandparents and great grandparents. Not just to confirm that they are super-friendly, well behaved and well trained but also, to check if they are still alive and healthy. In many cases, susceptibility to disease and injury is inherited. Thus, life expectancy is also inherited. To find potential problems in any line, don't waste too much time looking at show-quality dogs; you already know they are the picks of the litters. Instead, ask for names and addresses of pet owners who took the rest of the litters. Especially, try to track down pet dogs from litters born over 10 years ago.

Remember, longevity is the simplest, and often the best, indicator of good temperament, good behavior, good trainability and good

181

health. Save yourself a lot of heartbreak and pick a puppy from a line of dogs which all live to be canine senior citizens.

## Puppy Shots

Until pups have been immunized against the more serious canine diseases, they should not be allowed to mix with other dogs. Neither should they be allowed to frequent areas that may be contaminated by canine urine and feces. Canine Distemper may be contracted by sniffing urine from an infected animal, and similarly, Parvovirus and other infections are passed in canine feces. Moreover, these viruses are extremely virulent and may survive for a long time in both extreme heat and cold.

The immunization of young pups poses a bit of a problem. Newborn pups have passive immunity from maternal antibodies received in the colostrum, (the first milk after whelping). The level of maternal antibodies in young pups usually begins to decline around 6-8 weeks and passive immunity has disappeared by 9-12 weeks of age. Passive immunity may interfere with puppy shots which are given too early. Because of the uncertainty of the time when maternal antibodies have completely disappeared, it is normal practice for veterinarians to give a series of at least three injections, at intervals of 2-4 weeks commencing as early as six weeks of age. This practice is to stimulate immunity as soon as possible; it is not a ploy to increase veterinary fees. Adequate active immunity usually does not develop until about 12 weeks of age, i.e., within two weeks following the second injection given when maternal antibodies are no longer present.

Thus, your puppy is highly susceptible to life-threatening diseases from the time passive maternal immunity wanes until such time as the pup's own antibodies provide adequate protection. As such, between the ages of 6-12 weeks, great care should be taken to prevent your pup from coming into contact with potentially infected dogs and/or their urine and feces, i.e., during this time, your puppy should definitely not be allowed on sidewalks or in other public property.

It would be beneficial to hold training classes with puppies much younger than three months, but it just is not worth the risk. Before that time, you may train your puppy at home and hold regular puppy parties at home to socialize your pup with people. This is an opportune time to concentrate on puppy/people socialization. However, socialization, play and training with other puppies and dogs should be put on hold until your pup is at least three months of age and has developed good immunity against the more serious doggy diseases.

## Nutrition

These days, feeding a dog is an easy matter because the pet food industry has boomed into a multi-billion dollar business. A wide variety of excellent prepackaged dog foods are available in pet stores. The biggest advantage of feeding a commercial brand of dog food is convenience - an easy way of dispensing daily rations of a well balanced diet. However, the convenience of feeding commercial food is not without cost. Indeed, the biggest disadvantage is the expense - the two most expensive ingredients are the packaging and those cute advertisements on television; the individual ingredients represent only a fraction of the retail cost. Dry kibble in 50lb. bags is cheaper than moist canned food or individual servings.

Home-prepared menus offer an alternative to commercial dog foods. A diet based solely on human table scraps is generally not a good idea. But it depends on the human diet and the dog's alimentary constitution. Few people can prepare a healthy diet for themselves, and feeding leftovers to the dog is similarly unhealthy. So many pet dogs end up with livers like geese, kidneys like pebbles and bodies like turgid tomatoes. The dog is being slowly poisoned by the owner - too much food and especially too much fat, protein, calcium and sodium.

Some owners maintain home-prepared menus offer a more economical, healthier diet. Home-prepared food is certainly cheaper, but the preparation takes a lot of time. Certainly, the quality of some individual ingredients in home concoctions are better than those in lower quality generic dog foods, but the balance of ingredients is seldom as healthy. The correct balance of nutrients is equally as important as their quality. It is an extremely complicated process to produce a dog food with the correct proportions of carbohydrates, protein and fats, let alone the essential minerals, trace elements and vitamins. It is unlikely many dog owners can produce a home menu which is superior or better balanced than a premium brand dog food. I would suggest buying dry kibble in bulk and occasionally adding leftovers, including lots of vegetables, a moderate amount of carbohydrates and only a little lean meat.

Many dog owners feed too much food. Obesity is disastrous for the dog's health, especially for a middle-aged or geriatric dog. The two best indicators of food intake are your dog's waistline and the consistency of its stools. Make a habit of regularly weighing your dog each week and always weigh out its daily allotment of kibble each day. (This is especially important if more than one person feeds the dog. To avoid extra feedings, place the daily diet in a capped container.) If your dog looks too fat, weigh out less food each day and/or exercise the dog more. If your dog looks too thin, provide more food each day.

A good stool should resemble a rich brown, miniature, moist presto log. Overfeeding and/or dairy products generally cause loose stools, or diarrhea. Reduce the diet and/or substitute some dog food with boiled white rice. Constipated-concrete or sticky stools are the product of excess bones, fat and meat products.

Young puppies need to be fed little and often - usually three times a day. By the time they are four months old, they can get by on two meals a day. At six months, the dog may be fed once a day, or the owner may decide to continue feeding breakfast and supper. If in doubt, consult your veterinarian or pet store owner - that's why they are there.

## Grooming and Physical Examinations

By 'grooming' we do not necessarily mean that the dog is beautifully bathed, cutely coiffured and dressed up like a Christmas tree but rather, regular vigorous brushings and gentle combings. The primary purpose of grooming is to promote the vitality of the dog's skin and coat by ensuring that both are kept clean and healthy. There is no reason why a dog should not be clipped and wear ribbons, but the cosmetic reasons of grooming are only secondary. Bear in mind a very large proportion of veterinary visits will be for dermatological reasons and so, keep your dog's coat healthy.

A vigorous brushing helps massage your dog's skin and stimulate the blood supply. This helps reduce the incidence of 'hotspots' and other skin infections and inflammations. In addition, regular combing is by far the best flea control. Combing with a fine-toothed metal flea-comb not only removes the flea fodder - dander, dried, dead skin and old hairs but also, the fleas themselves. Captured fleas may be drowned in a cup of soapy water, He! He! He!

Grooming provides an opportunity to check your dog for other ectoparasites (ticks and mites), 'foxtails' (pointed and barbed dried grass seeds), and any cuts, bruises and lumps. You should make a point of examining your puppydog at least once a day. It is advisable to give the dog a once-over each time it comes in from outdoors. Don't forget to look in your dog's mouth, eyes, ears, nose and examine the dog's rear-end. A perfunctory grooming can save some large veterinary bills if, for example, 'foxtails' are removed before they enter the skin. Check to see if the teeth or ears are dirty and if the nails are too long. Clean the pup's teeth regularly, by gently rubbing with a damp cloth. It is vital to keep the gum-line clean and healthy, otherwise the soft, yellowy gunk will solidify into concrete-hard tartar, which will need to be chipped away to prevent gum disease and foul breath. Provide your dog with ample chewtoys. Personally, I like long bones and hard rubber Kong toys. If your dog's ears are dirty, gently clean them with a warm, moist cloth. With longhaired dogs that have long, hangy-down ears, trim the hair on the inside of the ear flap to improve air circulation and prevent infection. There is nothing worse than the smell of infected ears. If the nails are too long, clip them, and then, make a resolution to exercise the dog more.

In addition to the obvious medical advantages of regular inspections, frequent handling and gentling of the young pup helps build confidence so that it is more tractable when handled. Also, you will develop confidence and expertise in handling your dog. Feed your pup oodles of treats during examination. Right from the outset, get your pup to thoroughly enjoy being examined by family members and friends. This will make a trip to the veterinarian easier on the veterinarian, easier on your check-book, and easier on the dog. Nothing is worse than seeing a sick or injured dog further stressed when examined by the veterinarian, who is only trying to help the dog. Help your own dog - prepare it for visits to the veterinarian.

## Flea Control

Unless you live at high, flealess elevations, you will invest a great deal of time and money fighting with fleas. You will waste even more time and money trying to control fleas on dogs if you do nothing to control fleas in the dog's environment, i.e., your home. In both urban and rural areas, many fleas have developed a tolerance for extremely powerful insecticides. Many of these products are far too strong to use with young puppies or cats. Also, they should never be used if pregnant women or children are in the house.

The flea spends more time off the dog than on it. Only the adult flea makes itself at home on the dog. Even so, adult fleas can survive in the environment for over four months without feeding. As fast as fleas are eradicated on the dog, more fleas jump on. Female fleas feed for a couple of days and then commence laying hundreds and hundreds of eggs, which are scattered around your home and garden each time your dog scratches and shakes. The flea eggs fall into nooks and crannies, and within a few weeks, the baby fleas become adults and just can't wait to return home and live with Mum, on your warm woolly dog.

The success of flea control depends on regularly treating your dog's environment and regularly treating your dog. Again, regular brushings and combings are the best way to treat your dog. Thorough and regular use of the vacuum cleaner is by far the best way to keep your house free from eggs, larvae and adult fleas. After cleaning the house, vacuum up some flea powder to kill the fleas in the vacuum bag. Otherwise a vacuum bag filled with dog dander and dried, dead skin provides a scrumptious smorgasbord for young flealings, and in just a matter of days, a new generation of robust, healthy fleas will emerge, hopping down the vacuum tube in full saltatorial splendor, questing for a nice warm-blooded, furry home.

Remember to apply flea powder or sprays to your dog's favorite resting places in the yard, especially right outside the back door. Additionally, your dog must be treated each time that it comes indoors. Routinely groom your dog each time after returning from walks. If you have a back yard, train your dog to lie down on a mat by the door each time that it comes inside. Keep the mat regularly sprayed or powdered. In this fashion your dog will treat itself each time it comes inside. Once a week, vacuum and/or wash the dog's mat and apply fresh flea products.

Flea control is important, since fleas are the intermediate host of the dog tape worm, which infect the dog when it eats fleas. If your dog has fleas, it will probably need to be de-wormed as well. Flea infestation also may give rise to anemia and a variety of skin infections and inflammations, including 'hotspots' and allergic dermatitis. In addition, some fleas bite some humans.

## Castration and Spaying

Castrating male dogs (removing the testicles) and spaying bitches (removing the ovaries and uterus) render the animals sterile, preventing them from contributing to the already bulging pet population. For goodness sakes, if you are not thinking of breeding your dog, get it neutered right away. There are more than enough puppies and dogs to go around. Just go to your local animal shelter or humane society, and take a look. Approximately 10 million dogs are euthanized in U.S. humane societies each year, i.e., an estimated 20% of the dog population is euthanized annually! That's one every 3.2 seconds! And the dogs' only crime? They were born. A common misconception is that these pups are produced exclusively by irresponsible 'puppy mills'. Nope! The vast majority are produced by owners that want their male dog or bitch to participate in producing 'just one litter'. Well, the sum total of these 'just one litters' is colossal. It is difficult to grasp the sheer enormity of the problem, because the numbers are so mind-boggling. But to help you out, during the time it took you to read this paragraph 15 more dogs went to their death! Please neuter your dog.

If you still have your heart set on breeding your dog, just consider that raising a litter of pups is an extremely expensive, time-consuming pandemonium. As any good dog breeder will tell you, it absolutely wrecks your life and sleep for a full two months. Before allowing your male dog to experience the 'thrill' of mating, before volunteering your bitch to experience the 'joy' of giving birth, just make sure the product of this union - the puppies - have the certainty of experiencing the 'joys' of life!

If still in doubt, volunteer at the humane society to assist in the euthanasia of just one healthy, young pup. This will quickly put things in perspective. One moment, the pup is alive and happily squirming and wriggling in your grasp, trustingly licking your hand, and three seconds later, it is limp, lifeless, strangely heavy... and DEAD! Please neuter your dog.

## Spaying

There is much confusion concerning the physiological and behavioral effects of spaying. Some people feel that spaying will prompt a marked personality change and cause the bitch to become fat and ugly. Spaying has no deleterious effects on the bitch's personality whatsoever. If anything it makes her more predictable, relaxed and amenable - a better companion. It is true that oestrous hormones cause a reduced food intake and higher general activity, and since spaying removes the source of ovarian hormones, spayed bitches may tend to eat slightly more and exercise slightly less. However, you may easily rectify this situation by exercising your bitch a bit more and/or feeding her a bit less!

If you are not going to breed your bitch, have her spayed as soon as possible, and avoid potential complicated and costly obstetrical problems later in her life. A bitch with ovaries and uterus intact stands a progressively increasing risk of developing pyometra (pus in the uterus) as she gets older. It is far safer and cheaper to opt for a routine elective ovariohysterectomy now, than to risk the possibility of an extremely expensive, emergency and life-threatening operation when she is older.

## Castration

People seem to have numerous hang-ups about castrating male dogs. No doubt a psychologist could have a field day with the owner's projections and complexes. Castration does not make dogs more lethargic. If anything, a castrated dog is more attentive and willing to please its owner, since it is less distracted. Neither does castration cause a marked personality change. And castration does not make a dog a wimp.

The behavioral endocrinology of dogs is quite unique. Whereas the castration of most mammals appears to eliminate secondary sexual characteristics, the masculine characteristics of dog behavior appear to be emancipated from adult hormone levels. Whether or not a male dog will lift his leg when urinating, sniff and mount bitches and be more aggressive than females has all been preprogrammed by fetal testosterone in utero. Adult

*Castrated dogs skip better and soar higher*

castration has absolutely no direct effect on urination posture, sexual preference or hierarchical rank.

Castration does, however, exert a number of extremely beneficial behavioral changes. Castrated males tend to roam less than intact males. They are more content when left at home or in the yard and are less likely to develop destructive behaviors or attempt escape. A castrated dog will still urine-mark, using the characteristic male leg-lift posture, but it will do so less often.

Most importantly, castrated male dogs are involved in far fewer fights than their male counterparts with testicles. All dogs have disagreements, and most dogs fight. However, over 90% of dog fights occur between uncastrated male dogs. Strangely enough, castration does not make dogs less inclined to fight, neither does it reduce the dog's social standing vis a vis other dogs. Instead, castration reduces the desire for other dogs to pick fights with your dog. Castration removes the source of testosterone, the male sex hormone which makes male dogs smell male. Thus, castrated males appear to be less of a threat to other males, which consequently will be less aggressive and combative towards your dog. In a sense, castration makes your dog appear to be less obnoxious to others. Furthermore, if other dogs are more relaxed around your dog, your dog will feel more relaxed around them, and thus, he will be much easier to control.

*Well, thanks for your time. Bye Now! Gotta Go...*

## READING LIST

*Train Your Dog The Lazy Way* . Andrea Arden.
New York:Macmillan 1998.

*Owner's Guide To Better Behavior In Dogs*. William Campbell.
Loveland CO: Alpine Publications, Inc. 1989.

*The Culture Clash*. Jean Donaldson.
Oakland CA: James & Kenneth Publishers, 1996

*Doctor Dunbar's Good Little Dog Book*. Ian Dunbar.
Oakland CA: James & Kenneth Publishers, 1992

*Behavior Booklets: Preventing Aggression; Housetraining; Chewing: Digging; Barking; Socialization; Fighting; Fearfulness*. Ian Dunbar & Gwen Bohnenkamp.
Oakland CA: James & Kenneth Publishers, 1985.

*Don't Shoot the Dog!* Karen Pryor.
North Bend: Sunshine Books 1984

*Excel-Erated Learning!* Pamela Reid.
Oakland CA: James & Kenneth Publishers, 1996

*How To Raise A Puppy You Can Live With*. Clarice Rutherford & David Neil. Loveland CO: Alpine Publications, 1982.

*Help! This Animal is Driving Me Crazy!* Daniel Tortora.
Fireside, New York 1977

## WATCHING LIST

*Sirius Puppy Training*. Ian Dunbar.
Oakland CA: James & Kenneth Publishers, 1987.

*Dog Training For Children*. Ian Dunbar.
Oakland CA: James & Kenneth Publishers, 1996

*Training Dogs With Dunbar: Fun Training For You And Your Dog*. Ian Dunbar.
Oakland CA: James & Kenneth Publishers, 1996

*Training The Companion Dog* Ian Dunbar. (Set of 4 videos).
Oakland CA: James & Kenneth Publishers, 1992

*HOW TO TEACH A NEW DOG OLD TRICKS*

## SIRIUS® Puppy Training video

*The video which changed dog training!*

Before Sirius® there were *NO* puppy classes. Sirius® redefined and revolutionized dog training, by popularizing the use of lures and rewards and fun and games. Sirius® was the *original* puppy training video and it is still...

*...the leader of the pack!*

Learn the gentle and enjoyable off-leash training and socialization methods which made the SIRIUS® philosophy the hallmark of dog-friendly, companion dog training.

*VHS - 90 mins $29.95*

### DOG TRAINING FOR CHILDREN Video

All family members should learn how to train the family dog, especially children. This video helps children master a few simple training techniques to help them maximize their natural talents and prove that...

*...dog training is indeed child's play!*

Topics include: Taking on a new puppy; House training; Early lead training; Teaching sit and down; Developing a rapport; Focussing attention; Improving off-leash control; Training a fast recall; Improving the sit stay; Teaching with toys and playing training games.

*84 minutes $24.95*

## SIRIUS® Puppy Training classes

*Dog-friendly training to make people-friendly dogs*

For classes in California, New York and Hawaii, please call:

**(510) 658-8588  (800) 419-8748** (SF Bay Area);

(212) 213-4288 (Manhattan)  (808) 732-0258 (Honolulu)

Or, for dog training in your area contact:

*The Association of Pet Dog Trainers*
# 1- (800) PET DOGS

From the British television program:

# Dogs With Dunbar

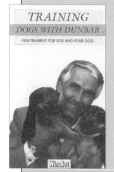

## TRAINING DOGS WITH DUNBAR Video

Dog training is not just about control; it's about relationships. If you have a good relationship with your dog, it will do its best to please you. So, make sure you use kind, patient and dog-friendly training techniques to enhance that relationship and produce a well mannered and loving companion. Dr. Dunbar's easy and enjoyable lure/reward methods make training fun for you and your dog.

65 minutes $24.95

## *Dr. Dunbar's* GOOD LITTLE DOG BOOK

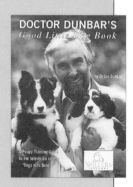

A truly wonderful, compendious puppydog training guide, outlining a gentle, practical approach. Delightfully written and beautifully illustrated with numerous sequential colour photographs. Contains a wealth of useful advice and ingenious tips for the prevention of common problems.

New 2nd Edition 68pp $15.00

## TRAINING THE COMPANION DOG Videos

A set of four specially edited videos based on the popular British television program, *Dogs With Dunbar* - filmed at a stately home in the enchanting New Forest area of England.

Vol. 1: Socialization & Early Training; Vol. 2: Behavior Problems; Vol. 3: Following & Walking On Leash and Vol 4: Recalls & Stays.

VHS - 60 minutes $25.00 each; $85.00 for set of four

# *Dog Aggression* videos

Veterinarian and animal behaviorist Dr. Ian Dunbar addresses the two most worrying behavior problems any dog owner can face - *dogs that bite and dogs that fight!*

Dealing effectively with canine aggression necessitates a comprehensive understanding of its underlying causes. In his characteristically entertaining and enlightening style, Dr. Dunbar offers a thoughtful analysis of why dogs bite, outlining numerous common-sense preventative measures and a variety of practical remedial training techniques. Dr. Dunbar's goal is to make *every dog a friendly dog.*

## BITING

Topics include: The relative influence of nature and nurture on the development of aggression. An in-depth review of the many stimuli and situations that may provoke a dog to bite. How to recognize warning signs and how to defuse potential triggers. A comprehensive classification of dog bites on the basis of severity and owner's responsibility. A suggestion for fairer, more effective legal sanctions. But most important: A detailed program of simple and effective behavior modification and temperament training techniques to prevent dog bites.

90 minutes $24.95

## FIGHTING

Topics include: The causes of dog-dog aggression in the context of pack hierarchy. How to assess whether a dog has a serious and dangerous fighting problem or whether it is just prone to squabbling. How castration defuses aggressive encounters. How to set up a remedial "growl class." How to use precise timing, rewards and reprimands to reduce and phase out aggression and build up a dog's confidence and social savvy.

65 minutes $24.95

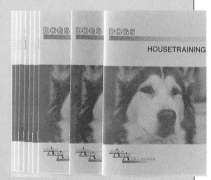